AF564402

The Soul of India

A Constructive Study of Indian Thoughts and Ideals

Bipin Chandra Pal

First LG Edition 2017
Reprinted 2019
Reprinted 2025

ISBN 978–93–83723–21–8

Published by
LG PUBLISHERS DISTRIBUTORS
49, Street No. 14, Pratap Nagar
Mayur Vihar Phase I, Delhi 110091
lgpdist@gmail.com

Printed at
D.K. Fine Art Press, Delhi

BIPIN CHANDRA PAL

Born : November 7, 1858 Died : May 20, 1932

ॐ

इहा आमि किछुइ ना जानि
ये तुमि कहाओ सेइ कहि आमि वाणी
तोमार शिक्षाय पड़ि येन शुक पाठ,
साक्षात् ईश्वर तुमि, के वुझे तोमार नाट ?
हृदये प्रेरण कर, जिह्वाय कहाओ वाणी ;
कि कहिब भालमन्द, किछुइ ना जानि ।

—चैतण्य महाप्रभु प्रति रामानन्द वाक्यम् ।

चैः चः मध्यलीला, ८म पः

Om.

Nought excepting this I know
That what from my lips doth flow
Is what thou bid'st me say.

And what I pour from out my throat
Parrot-like I learnt by rote
From thee Lord, each day.

A present God thou art, and none
Can fathom what by thee is done
In sport or playful mood.

This heart with thoughts thou e'er dost fill
This tongue with speech providest still
I know not ill or good.

CONTENTS

LETTER I

FUNDAMENTAL CONSIDERATIONS

			PAGE
Personal and Prefatory	...	...	1
English Works on India	...	...	3
Interpretation of India by Orientalists		...	4
Missionary Presentations	...	...	5
Works by Anglo-Indian Officials	...	...	7
Misleading not Dishonest	...	...	8
An Interpretation of the Eucharist	...	...	9
European Interpretation of our 'Nakedness'		...	10
As the Blind Saw the Elephant	...	...	12
As the Fishes Knew the Sea	...	...	13
The Recorder and the Interpreter	...	...	14
Another Hindu Story	...	...	15
Differece Between the European and the Indian		...	16
The Greek and the Hindu	...	...	17
The Pursuit of the Universal	...	...	20
The Peculiarity of the Greek Mind	...	...	21
The European Temperament	...	...	22
The Peculiarity of the Hindu Mind	...	...	22
The Indian Temperament	...	...	23
The Different Standards of Values	...	...	24
The Spoilt Child of Modern Humanity		...	26
Sister Nivedita	...	...	28
An Old Hindu Canon of Art	...	...	30
True Nirvana—What It Means	...	...	31
Baba Arjoondas	...	...	32
Another Holy Man	...	...	35
An Actual Superman	...	...	37
Pandit Bijay Krishna Goswami	...	...	38
The True Indian Prototype	...	...	42
Characteristics of the Indian Ideal	...	...	45
Dharma—The Basis of Our Civilisation		...	46

LETTER II

THE NAME AND THE THING

Personal and Prefatory 50
The True Interpreter 50
The Reformer and The Reactionary 52
India as Seen by the Stranger 57
India—A Mere Geographical Expression ... 58
The Popular Anglo-Indian View 61
India as Known to Her Own Children ... 62
Meaning of Geographical Names 63
The Meaning of Bharatavarsha 64
The Character of Indian Unity 66
Aryan Expansion in India 70
The Nature of the Old Aryan Propaganda ... 73
Varnasrama-Dharma or the Caste-and-Order law ... 75
The Ashrama-Law 82
Aryan Methods of Unification 84
Hindu India 87
Mahomedan India 89

LETTER III

INDIA: THE MOTHER

Cultural Unity and National Unity 94
The Old Indian Type—Federal 100
Characteristics of Western Patriotism 101
The Hindu Ideal of Patriotism 103
Mother and Motherland 104
The Nature Gods of the Hindus 105
Hindu Theory of Ultimate Reality 108
Christian Trinity and Hindu Purusha-Prakriti ... 110
Christ and Prakriti 112
Prakriti as Maya, Radha and Shakti ... 114
The Problem of Personality 116
Prakriti and Logos 117
The Being Behind Nationality 118
The Primal Form of The Mother 119

Shakti as Jagaddhatri 120
Shakti as Kalee 122
Shakti as Durga 123
The Nationalist Interpretation of Durga ... 127
The History of the Durga Cult 130
The New Patriotism 132

LETTER IV

RELIGIOUS INDIA

Budhism and Hinduism 140
Hinduism—Not a Creed but a Culture ... 142
Hindu Pantheism 144
What is the "Thou" 145
"The Witness" in Us 147
The Key to The Hindu Religion 149
The Scientific Character of Hinduism ... 149
The Bhrigu-Varuna Episode 150
Hinduism—A Culture, not a Creed 156
The Universal Reference of the Bhrigu-Varuna Episode 157
Physical Purity: Cleanliness 161
"Instructive" and "Constructive" 164
The Ethics of Psycho-Physics 167
Moral Education 173
The Education of the Will 176
Mastery Over Nature 180
Idolatry or Idea-latry 186
Gods and Goddesses as Superior Spiritual Beings ... 192
The Krishna-Cult 197
The "Form" of Krishna 203
Personality of the Absolute 209
The Three Gunas 211
Man Becomes Divine 214
Two Aspects of Leela 216
The Nine Rasas 221
Vaishnavic Contribution to Hindu Æsthetics ... 223

Om

Shree Shree Guravè Namah

LETTER I

FUNDAMENTAL CONSIDERATIONS

Personal and Prefatory

I am sincerely thankful that you are not coming out to India this season. You will, perhaps, think it cruel of me to be so glad at what must have been a sore disappointment to you. But though I did not actually discourage you, I never really liked the idea of your coming to see us just yet. The time is not yet, my child, when you could profitably come face to face with our life and institutions. There is as yet a very large element of poetic fancy in your admiration for India. You have read something of our past history and achievements and have been profoundly impressed with the grandeur of our ancient civilisation. Indeed, it is a commonplace of present-day European thought, to speak in high terms of our past. Even Mr. Theodore Roosevelt could not refuse to admit that we were highly civilised at one time, though that high and ancient civilisation has somehow "gone crooked" in our day. This is the general European estimate of modern India. I know you strongly resented the flighty utterances of the ex-American President. But yet I am not sure whether even to yòu, direct and living contact with our present life and habits would not come as something of a rude shock. Few Europeans have had a greater love and regard for Indian thought and life than the late Prof. Max Muller. Yet even Max Muller refused all through his life to come out to India, lest his idealism should be destroyed by our present day actualities. Max Muller's appreciation was essentially intellectual. Yours, I know, is much deeper ; it is spiritual. It is the special privilege of your sex to seize the spiritual where we, mere men, even at our best, can rarely go beyond the intellectual. But still even you require a further period of aloofness and training to be able to truly enter into the inner spirit of our complex life and culture. This is why I am glad that you are not coming out to India so soon. Cherish your virgin romance religiously. Seek not, my child, to lift the veil off the face of this Beautiful Mystery before the due term of your novitiate is over. I want you to come to us not as a tourist, nor as a mere student but as a pilgrim, in love and reverence ; for it is only then that you will be able to know what India is to-day, what she was in the past, and what, in the providence of God, she must be in the near future, to be able to fulfil her divinely-ordained mission to that Universal Humanity towards which, consciously or unconsciously, the nations of the world are moving so fast in our time.

English Works on India

You want to know what books I would recommmend to you to help you in your further study and understanding of our life and thought. Truth to say, there is not one that I know of which I would wish you to read now. There is no dearth of English books on India. They are the works of Anglo-Indian officials and European tourists. Every publishing season in London and New York is adding to their number. I cannot say that I have read them all. But in a general way I am fairly acquainted with the character of these books, and I may say without offence that none of these reveal the real soul of India. Their authors are not to blame for it. Most of them have done their best. And it is not their fault that they had not the right key for opening our door.

These books may be broadly divided into three classes. The first deal largely with ancient India. They are written by European Orientalists, Max Muller and Monier Williams, Macdonald and Rhys Davis and others in our day. Sir William Jones, Horace Hayman Wilson and

Muir and others, in the early eighteenth century, have given to the English-speaking world the result of their lifelong studies in ancient Sanskrit literature or Indo-Aryan civilisation. Christian missionaries from the days of Carey, Marshman and Ward have tried frequently to discuss the religious life and institutions of our land. Anglo-Indian officials have also placed on record, now and again, their impressions and memories of the country where they spent the greater part of their active life. But I know not of one single book among all these that has seized the full truth and reality of our life and culture. The best of these are like Max Muller's "India : what it can teach us", the worst, I think, are like Sir J. D. Rees' "Real India."

Interpretation of India by Orientalists

Max Muller and other Orientalists know something, no doubt, of our past, and speak in terms almost of exaggerated admiration of that past. But almost invariably they leave the sad impression upon the reader's mind that all that they say are mere matters of ancient history, have an academic and antiquarian interest only, but no reference to the actualities of the present ; and that though India was, undoubtedly, highly civilised at a time when the puissant nations of the modern world had scarcely emerged out of primitive barbarism, the India of to-day is not only different from the India of the Vedas, the Upanishads or the great Epics, but has irretrievably fallen away from that high position. Max Muller was so keenly conscious of this pitiful disparity between ancient and modern India, that he persistently refused, as I have said, to come to this country, lest his dream-picture of our land and people should be cruelly destroyed. The fact of the matter really is that neither Max Muller nor any other European Orientalist has been able to seize the true course of historic evolution in India. Not one of them, so far as I know, has been able to grasp the truth that age after age, and epoch after epoch, there have been evolution and progress in India as elsewhere, that this process of progressive evolution was never stopped at any period of our history and it is going on as much to-day as it did at the time of the Vedas, the Upanishads or the Epics. And their failure to recognise this elementary fact has vitiated all their judgment of Indian life and civilisation.

Missionary Presentations

As regards the works of European Christian missionaries, these are generally of a contentious character, written with the natural prepossessions of the religious propagandist, and are, consequently, without any value as a correct exposition of our religious ideals and institutions. They have naturally applied the canons of Christianity to the interpretation of an apparently different order of religious experience and symbolism. There is, no doubt, a very close affinity between the deeper strains of Christain and Hindu thought. There is a high level of spiritual life and thought, where both the advanced Christian and the advanced Hindu, particularly of the Vaishnavic or Shaivite schools,—the schools of love and faith in Hinduism—speak of the same eternal truths, though in different languages and through their own peculiar symbols. Unfortunately, however, Christian propagandism in India, as, in fact, in every non-Christian land, has but little appreciation of these deeper affinities. The outer shells, the external symbols and the popular dogmas and rituals of these two great world-religions are what the ordinary, unillumined and unspiritual votaries of either recognise and know in the other. Naturally, therefore, the carnal conflicts of ununderstood dogmas and lifeless symbols have almost invariably vitiated the judgment of the ordinary unspiritual Hindu of the truth and reality of Christianity and that of the ordinary Christian propagandist of the truth and reality of Hinduism. Missionary presentations of Indian life and religion are not only unreliable, but are often even needlessly offensive to Indian susceptibilities.

Works by Anglo-Indian Officials

The third class of books, written by Anglo-Indian officials, generally deal with the particularities of official life and experience, and discuss present-day economic, social and administrative problems. The British officials in India, like the Christian missionaries, have also the peculiar prejudices and prepossessions of their own class and country. They are the children of modern Europe, steeped in the spirit of what is called modern civilisation, and even the ablest of them cannot help applying, in their study and judgment of Indian life and institutions, the generalisations of European history and culture. They have little or no consciousness of the fact that Indian experience belongs to a somewhat different order from that of Europe, and the generalisations of the one cannot be reasonably applied to the interpretation of the other. Besides, the India which British officials know most intimately is that which the introduction of English education and the superimpositon of British institutions, both economic and political, upon an ancient and civilized people, have created. They come face to face only with that side of our life and character which is open to official contact and alien influences. Behind and beyond this, there is our larger social and domestic life, and our still more large and deep religious and spiritual life. Of this the Anglo-Indian officials know little and understand even less. It is quite natural, tberefore, that they too, inspite of their long residence in the country and their intimate official connections with the people they rule, have failed, as much as the others, to enter into the inner spirit of our life and culture.

Misleading not Dishonest

But however imperfect and misleading their presentation of Indian life and culture may be, I do not by any means say or suggest that even the most incompetent of these European writers on India have been guilty of deliberate misrepresentation. They have tried to faithfully record what they have actually seen or heard. But they usually forget the common truth that what we see or hear are mere externals and appearances.

Sense-testimony is no doubt absolute on the physical plane. When, therefore, the European scientist studies the physical features of our land, when he mensurates our fields, trigonometrates our altitudes and undulations, investigates our animal, our vegetable or our mineral kingdoms, the records of his study and investigations are accepted as true and authoritative. But the study of man belongs altogether to a different plane. The specific organs of truth in the domain of the psychological, the sociological and the spiritual sciences are not our senses. Here also the eye sees, the ear hears ; but the real meaning of what is seen or heard is supplied not by the senses but by the understanding, which interprets what is seen or heard in the light of its own peculiar experiences and associations.

An Interpretation of the Eucharist

Ages ago, in the very infancy of the Christian era, a Hindu traveller went on a visit to some Christian colony, probably in Asia Minor. The story of this visit has been described in the Naradiya Upakhyana of the Sanskrit epic Mahabharata. We read here that the author of this Upakhyana came across a peculiar religious sect who "ate up the God they worshipped." Seen with the eye alone, it is a faithful description of the Christian sacrament of the Eucharist or the Holy Communion. The priest blesses the bread and wine placed on the Communion table. He mutters some prayers over these. He does so in an attitude of worship. To those who are used to the worship of the Deity through symbols or images, the Communion service would naturally appear as a worship of bread and wine.

And when the consecrated bread and wine are distributed among the congregation, they do appear to be "eating the God they worshipped." The writer saw from the outside; cognised with his senses certain physical acts of the Christian worshippers. He had not the right key to the interpretation of these outer acts. He put his own meaning on these in the light of his own peculiar experience. What he saw was a fact, yet how misleading is his interpretation of what he had seen! And the story illustrates very clearly the general character of the interpretations put upon our life and institutions by European scholars and sojourners.

European Interpretation of our "Nakedness"

A few months ago an eminent British journalist came out to India to study the present situation in the country. The very first thing that he communicated to the journal he represented was the disgusting nakedness of our people. Such nakedness is almost entirely unknown in Europe or America. Lack of decent clothing is associated there with squalid poverty, dirt and drink,—the result of intellectual inferiority or moral degeneration. People there have also read of the naked cannibal, in books of travel. The seminudity of our teeming populations is, therefore, naturally interpreted by the superficial

European observer as a proof of our semi-barbarism. He forgets, however, that people's dress, like the wool of animals, is determined, in the natural course of their evolution, almost entirely, by the climatic character of their habitat. Our short and thin loin-cloths and bare upper limbs as the general dress of our male population are almost a stern necessity in our sweating sweltry climate. Nature demands this of us. They are no more a proof of our barbarism than is the opera or ball dress of fashionable Western society,—which cannot even plead such natural necessity,—any proof of the lower culture or character of Europe. As with our national dress, so also with all our social or domestic institutions. They have had a long course of historic evloution behind them. Whatever their present moral or physical value, whether they be good or they be bad in the judgment of the modern man,—they owe their origin and development to imperious historic needs, grew out of the natural attempt of our social organism to adapt itself, from epoch to epoch, to its changing environment, both physical and social. And this being the case, they can only be rightly understood and interpreted in the light of our general history and culture. Unfortunately, however, few European writers on India get the right perspective of our history and evolution. They come from the outside. They carry with them all the prepossessions and prejudices of their own country and culture. They observe the externals of our life and institutions. And even the best of them see India as a company of blind people,—in the story cited in our logical text-books—"saw" the elephant.

As the Blind "Saw" the Elephant

The blind people of a village, so runs this old story, once went to see an elephant that had come to their neighbourhood. They were led near the animal, and standing around it, each man put out his hand to feel how it was like. One man stroked the trunk of the elephant, another its ear, a third its leg, a fourth its tail; and thus they "saw" the elephant. Coming home they commenced to describe the animal to their friends. The man who had stroked its trunk said that it was like a large python. He who had stroked its ear, contended that it was like an immense winnowing fan. He who had felt its leg swore that the elephant was like a huge pillar. What each of these blind men said was absolutely true so far as his own particular sense-knowledge went; yet how monstrously false it was as a picture of the elephant! Similarly what the European writers on India record is, in a sense, true so far as their own particular sense-impressions go. Yet it may be,—indeed most frequently is—all the same, monstrously false, as a picture of real India.

Some writers have seen only a particular Indian province, and have confidently presented the particularities of their limited and superficial experience as a general statement of truth about Indian life and civilisation. Others, with a wider range of experience, have been impressed with the endless varieties of our provincial and ethnic life and institutions, but have absoultely failed to seize the fundamental unity that stands behind these bewildering diversities. They have all seen India as the blind people in the story "saw" the elephant.

As the Fishes Knew the Sea

An Anglo-Indian official once declared that he had spent thirty years of the best part of his life in India, and claimed, therefore, to speak with the authority of a specialist on Indian history and civilisation. But he forgot that mere physical contact with a thing does not necessarily lead to a full and correct knowledge of it.

The fishes of the sea, so runs a Chinese story, once went in a body to the big, wise fish, and wanted to know what the sea was like. Yet they had lived all their life in that self-same sea. The story was evidently invented to drive home a fundamental theological truth, but may be repeated here to illustrate a very common Anglo-Indian error in regard to Indian life and institutions.

The Recorder and the Interpreter

The fact really is that even the oldest European residents in India can, as a class, claim only what may be called a mere sense-contact with our life and habits. Except under very exceptional circumstances, even neither much learning nor close research can help them to a more intimate veiw of our character and culture. For our senses can never take us beyond the apparent and the objective. The function of the senses is simply to record outer impressions, but not to interpret them. Even on the physical plane, while the records of phenomena come from the senses, their intelligent interpretation, which alone raises these to the position of science, is always supplied by the mind. In fact, the natural or the physical order with which our senses deal, is not absolutely sensuous either. Had it been so, our knowledge of physical phenomena would have belonged to the same class as that of the lower animals, would consist of isolated and unsystematised sense-impressions only. The physical sciences have been made possible upon the assumption that the outer and sensuous natural order does not stand by itself, but is correlated to our inner mental order, and, therefore, admits of being rightly interpreted in the terms of our thought or reason. But while there is a general agreement among men of equal intelligence and education, in regard to the interpretation of physical phenomena, there is no such agreement in regard to the interpretation of the more complex mental and spiritual experiences ; and the standard of judgment in regard to human activities and institutions is, therefore, fundamentally different from that which is applied to the interpretation of physical facts. Here the standard is essentially psychological and spiritual, determined by the character of the intellectual and socio-ethical life and ideals of the observer, and it widely differs in different persons, owing to differences in their mental temperament and training.

Another Hindu Story

Three men, so goes another popular Hindu story, once simultaneously heard the exclamation—"Alas ! the night is gone." One of them was a devotee, engaged in his early morning devotions ; the second a lover, in the company of his love ; and the third a burglar, prowling about for robbery. And these three men put three different interpretations upon this one simple exclamation ! The devotee thought,—"Here is a holy man, repenting the loss of so many precious hours of the night in sleep, which should have been spent in meditation and prayer." The lover thought,—"Here is another unfortunate person like myself whom the signs of breaking dawn are threatening with cruel separation from his love." The thief thought,—"Lo ! here is another poor burglar who have had, evidently, no chance to rob anybody to-night." We are all, whether ignorant or wise, like these people, always putting our own meaning, in the light of our special temperament or experience, upon men and things. The European does so in regard to things Indian ; even the Indian with much less excuse, in view of the peculiarly catholic, synthetic and universal spirit of his civilisation and culture, is doing the same in regard to things European. More than half of their mutual misunderstandings are due to this cause. They forget the fundamental difference, both of temperament and training, that exists between them.

Difference Between the European and the Indian

This difference may, I think, be best explained by a reference to the peculiar constitutions of the Hindu and the Greek mind. For these two ancient peoples may well be taken as typical of the two great world-cultures that India and Europe respectively represent. Indian culture is not absolutely Hindu, nor is the European culture absolutely Greek. Like all great world-cultures, they are both of a complex and composite character. Many races and many cultures have contributed to their growth and evolution. But still the main current of European culture has flowed from Greece and the central stream of Indian culture has flowed through the Hindu people. These two world-cultures have received their special features mainly from these two great divisions of the Aryan people.

The Greek and the Hindu

As members of the same race, there are, necessarily, many fundamental affinities between the Greek and the Hindu. Their physical structure is fundamentally the same. Generally speaking, the Hindu has the same regular features, the same straight or curly hair, the same shape of the cranium, as the Greek ; and whatever variations are observed between them today, whether in cut or in colour, are due to what the anthropologist calls miscegenation or mixture with other stocks. But all these differences notwithstanding, the original physical affinities between these two peoples are too marked to be ignored. Like their original physical structure, the fundamental social structure of these two peoples has also been the same. As in Greece, so also in India, the rudimentary structure both of the society and the state has always been constitutional and democratic, as distinguished from the military or despotic type of the Semitic races. Their thought-structure, as revealed by the structural peculiarities of their respective languages, is also the same. Language is the expression of thought, and the structure of a language is always determined by the structural peculiarities of the thought of the people among whom that language has been developed. The character of a people's mind is revealed by the position which is assigned in their grammar to the three elements of thought—subject, object and predicate. In the grammatical construction of some languages, the subject dominates the object, in some the object dominates the subject. The absolute domination of the subject over the object in the grammatical structure of any language indicates the essential character of the thought-life of the people by whom, from prehistoric times, that language has been spoken. And this domination means that in the thought of this people the consciousness of the subject or the self through which the consciousness of the Absolute is evolved and developed among every people, has always been very clear and pronounced.

The absolute dominance of the subject over the object is the common character of both Sanskrit and Greek. Nowhere outside the special family of languages, generally called Indo-Aryan, which includes Sanskrit and all the Sanskrit-derived vernaculars of India on the one hand, and Greek, Latin and the modern languages of Europe on the other,—nowhere outside this group, do we find anything similar to the significant construction "I am"—Sanskrit "Aham-asmi,"—indicating mere existence, simple being, without any reference to doing. And it shows that the sense of being as being, of the subject independent of the object, of the noumenon or the Absolute,—self-existent, self-conditioned, self-determined,—has been an original sense with these peoples. This is the peculiarity of the Aryan thought-structure. It is a most prominent feature of the Aryan race-consciousness. It is the true spiritual sense. It is common to both the Hindu and the Greek ; common, therefore, to both Indian and European cultures. This strange and rudimentary mental and spiritual affinity between the Greek and the Hindu is proved not merely by the structural similarity of Greek and Sanskrit, but equally also by the general character of all the later and more developed philosophies and arts of these two ancient peoples. Yet there was, inside this wide and fundamental unity, an equally fundamental difference also between their respective mental temperament and spiritual character.

The Pursuit of the Universal

Both the Greek and the Hindu, you will thus see, have had the same innate sense of the spiritual and the universal as an original endowment of their race-consciousness. This sense of the spiritual and the universal is everywhere expressed through man's perception of the whole. And the whole may be viewed in two ways : we may view it as a Concrete Reality, or as an Abstract Idea or Principle. In other words, we may view the whole *through* its parts, approach it through the mutual relations of parts to parts, and of the parts, both severally and collectively, to the whole of which they are parts. This is predominantly the way of science. Following this way, we ultimately arrive at what is called the Concrete Universal or the *Apara* or *Saguna* Brahman of the Hindus. We may also view the whole *in* the parts. In the true organic conception of the whole, while *actually* it is *revealed through* its parts *logically* it is equally *implied*, not partially but fully, *in* each one of these parts. The complete thought, though organised in a long and complete sentence, is, however, implicit in each of the words of it. It is the regulative idea that has determined the position of each of these words in the whole sentence. This is the universal character of all organic wholes. We may, therefore, equally seize the whole *in* its parts also. This is predominantly the way of metaphysics. Following this way, we ultimately arrive at what is called the Abstract Universal,—the *Para* or the *Nirguna* Brahman of our philosophy. And the pursuit of the Whole or the Absolute through these two different methods, develops two different types of mind.

The Peculiarity of the Greek Mind

In seeking to realise the whole *through* the parts, we have necessarily to develop and define the relations, both severally and collectively, of the parts to the whole of which they are parts. Those who have, from pre-historic times been used to the pursuit of the whole *through* the parts, have necessarily developed a particular mental temperament. In constantly seeking to seize and define the mutual relations of objects, their mind, as a matter of course, becomes pre-eminently definitive and analytic, objective and realistic. The Greek followed this way, and these are the distinctive characteristics of the Greek mind. Not that it had no subjectivity or idealism. Every analysis works towards a synthesis, every definition suggests a necessary integretion, and no apprehension of the real is really possible except upon a more or less conscious back-ground of the ideal. Greek thought was not, therefore, absolutely analytic or definitive or objective or realistic. Both realism and idealism were fully developed in the Greek consciousness. It harmonised the Concrete with the Abstract Universal, even as the Hindus did. But still the dominant emphasis was on the former, and not on the latter. *The* word of Greek culture is, therefore, Form or Definition.

The European Temperament

Modern Europe is the child of ancient Greece. The characteristic European temperament is fundamentally the same as the Greek temperament. The European mind, even in our own day is thus more prone to define and differentiate than to combine and integrate, more able to analyse than to synthesize ; it is more formal than transcendental, more scientific than metaphysical, more objective than subjective, more positive than imaginative, more realistic than idealistic.

The Peculiarity of the Hindu Mind

The Hindu, on the other hand, has, from pre-historic times, followed the opposite way.

He has pursued the whole not *through* but *in* the parts. And when we seek the whole *in* the parts, instead of developing we have to deny, instead of positing we have to negate, instead of recognising we have to ignore, the particularities of experience and train the mind to constantly transcend every form of definition and relativity, with a view to reach and realise the Undefinable and the Absolute. It is the way of metaphysics. The Hindu has always followed this way. Not that he never developed any science or philosophy, or that his intellect has been totally devoid of that definitiveness, characteristic of the Greek. Like the definitive Greek intellect, the Hindu intellect also developed most wonderful systems of grammar and rhetoric, logic and jurisprudence, and even a body of positive sciences at a time when it was scarcely known in Europe. His conception of the Concrete Universal or *Saguna* Brahman, is no less clear, though, perhaps, more full and philosophical, than that of the Greek. But still, the predominant emphasis of his thought has been more on the idealistic and the abstract than on the realistic and the concrete.

The Indian Temperament

The resulting mental temperament of the Hindu is, therefore, necessarily more transcendental than formal, more metaphysical than scientific, more imaginative than positive, more idealistic than realistic. And these two fundamentally different types of mental temperaments have created two quite different standards of intellectual and moral values among these two groups of mankind.

The Different Standards of Values

With the European, the standard of intellectual, moral and spiritual values is thus, more physical than mental, more external than internal, more sensuous than spiritual. If a European walks from one place to another, he will measure the distance in the terms of miles and furlongs. If he stands before a mountain he will scan its altitude by the theodolite, and express it in relation to the sea-level. If he sees a human being he will psychometrate him, with a view to know his exact proportions. The European can scarcely study even supersensuous facts and experiences except through some sensuous and external help. He seeks to study man's intelligence by measuring his cranium and weighing his brains ; and deduces all his highest generalisations regarding the intellectual or moral advancement of nations and communities from outer statistics and averages. His intellect cannot be satisfied unless all the details, which means the particularities of an object, are clearly seized and sized and put in their proper place and pose. Even when he rises to the perception of the general he does so by laboriously climbing through the particulars. In the examination or presentation of a thing or theme, neglect of these particularities is to the European an unpardonable intellectual fault.

The Hindu, however, has quite a different standard of intellectual, moral and spiritual values. If he walks from one place to another, he would oftentimes measure the distance not by chain and compass, but by his own muscles and nerves, and will report it in the terms of his own sensation and emotion. Sometimes, therefore, walking a mile to meet his friend or lover, he will say that he only walked a few steps ; on another occasion, when dragged by unpleasant duty or external necessity out of his home to his near neighbour, he would perhaps say that he walked a mile. His standard of values is internal not external, intellectual not physical, emotional and not rational in the usual narrow sense of these terms. By temperament he has an instinctive and intense distaste of details. By heredity and training he knows only how to seize the universal to the apparent neglect of isolated particulars. What the European, judging by his own objective and particularistic standard of intellectual, moral or spiritual values, condemns as exaggerations of the Oriental mind are, therefore, really no exaggerations at all, but are simply the results of a different standard of values. Occasionally even the positive and practical European also adopts this Hindu standard. When a friend meeting a friend after a few weeks says—"I have not seen you for ages,"—he really, neither exaggerates nor lies but simply applies his own inner emotional standard to the measurement of outer time. Ordinarily, in regard to events which have little or no reference to his deeper emotions, the European measures time by the swing of the pendulum in his hall-clock. But when his soul is stirred by some deep emotion, whether of love or hatred, then even he ignores perforce his habitual standard of outer and objective values, and seizes his own inner self as the only true measure of time, space and all things besides. And what is thus as yet merely occasional and momentary in the European, is a habitual and permanent characteristic of the Hindu mind ; this is really all the difference between them.

The Spoilt Child of Modern Humanity

I am trying to point out these fundamental psychological differences in the very constitution of the European and the Indian, to explain to you the reason why, in spite of their high education and superior intelligence, even the very best of the European residents or students of India have, almost invariably, failed to truly understand or interpret us. Added to these intellectual difficulties, there are equally serious moral disabilities under which the European student of Indian character and culture labours. The European is the spolit child of modern humanity. Everybody is humouring him. All the world is praising his wonderful intelligence and acquisitions. Even those who try to verbally deny his superiority, really admit it, by seeking, with all their might, to imitate his ways. He criticises every other culture and civilisation, few have had the temerity to criticise his. He lays down the law of modern life and progress for others but no one has as yet been able to gather up sufficient courage or conceit to lay it down for him. He has sent out his missionaries for the conversion of the world, no one has similarly tried to proseletyze him. All these things have created a strong sense of his own superiority in the European, And this conceit of unquestioned superiority absolutely incapacitates the European in having a correct understanding of world-cultures different from his own. He recognises these differences. He admits that—

The East is East and the West is West
And the twain ne'er shall meet.

But all the same, he persistently prefers his own standard of values, as the universal standard by which all the world must be judged. And his claim to interpret us, inspite of this acknowledged difference, means only the claim of the higher, in organic evolution, to explain and interpret the meaning and purpose of the lower !

But if the East be not in reality only a less developed West, and if there be any truth in the statement that—

The East is East and the West is West

—in other words, if the difference between the very constitutions and structures of these two sections of mankind be so fundamental as to seem almost as a difference in kind, then, the only possibility of the one to truly understand the other, must lie in its ability to mentally detach itself from itself, and through the exercise of a highly-developed representative imagination, to spiritually identify itself with the subject of its study and interpretation. But few Europeans have as yet been able to do so.

Sister Nivedita

The only exception that I know of, was the late Miss Margaret Noble, known and loved all over India, in her adopted name of Sister Nivedita, of the Order of Ramkrishna and Vivekananda. Nivedita's self-effacemet was almost complete. Even few Indians, especially of the modern-educated classes, have as yet been inspired by so all-consuming a passion for India, as transfigured this British woman. Nivedita came to us, as no European had as yet come, not as an adept but as a novice ; not as a teacher but as a learner. She did not pose before us as a prophetess but always stood, in sincere love and reverence, as a worshipper. She had no ambition to play the *role* of the high-priestess of any new or old cult. She never claimed any sanctified privilege nor any position of special honour. But in the exuberance of her virgin love for the soul of India, a glimpse of which had been revealed to her by her Guru or Master, she came simply to lose herself in us, and by so losing herself, to find herself back, per chance, as a true seer of our spirit and culture. And her unique devotion to our land and people had its reward in the almost complete understanding of some aspects at least of our life and institutions that was vouchsafed unto her. She had, my child, if I am not mistaken, a touch of your own blood in her, and the quick intellectual perceptions and broad spiritual sympathies ot her Irish heritage enabled her to see the true soul of

India, where the unimaginative and unsympathetic Englishman or American could hardly peer beyond the outermost covering of her divine body. In her "Web of Indian Life", Sister Nivedita has presented a more correct interpretation of some aspects of our present-day life and thought than is found in any other English book on India that I know of.

An Old Hindu Canon of Art

The fact of the matter is that no one can correctly interpret anything without himself becoming that thing. It is true not only of the interpretation of men, but even of animals and vegetables. This truth had been seized ages ago by us, and it is an old canon of Hindu art that to correctly draw or paint an object, the artist must first himself be that object ; for, the true function of the painter's or the sculptor's art is not merely to reproduce with absolute fidelity the forms of things, which may very well be done by any trained photographer, but to reveal their inner soul or being. And the complete mental and spiritual identification of the artist with his subject is the only way to reach this ideal. To correctly present India, one must therefore first be himself an Indian, not merely by birth but in heart and spirit. But such self-effacement is almost impossible of attainment by the ordinary

European ; for the European, my child, can never cease to be a European, nay not even in imagination.

True Nirvana—What It Means

It has however been very different with the Hindu. A most porwerful and unique representative imagination has been the special heritage of our people. It is the fruit of our age-long social and spiritual disciplines. To kill the conceit of self as a thing apart and thus to seize the universal everywhere,—this has been the one eternal objective or all our evolution and culture. Our rituals and sacraments, our fasts and feasts, our social regulations and religious liturgies, all have from time immemorial this one end in view, namely, the realisation of the Absolute through the conscious spiritual identification of the individual self with the universal. Our highest conception of salvation is therefore called *Brahma-nirvana*, which means not the annihilation of self-consciousness but only the conscious and spiritual identification of the individual with the universal through transending all the carnal limitations of the human as human. The true *Yogi*, says Sree Krishna in the Bhagavat-Geeta, "sees the self (his own self) in all things, and sees all things in the self", and losing the conceit of independent and isolated personality he attains the vision of the Universal.

"He who sees Me everywhere, and
sees everything in Me,
I never pass out of his sight, nor
does he ever pass out of Mine."

This is the true and positive conception of *nirvana.* It is a universal Hindu ideal. Realising the identity of his own self with the Universal, the sage Bamadeva, we are told in the Vedas, declared : "I am the sun, I was Manu." Every true Hindu devotee pursues this self-same ideal even today, and some at least actually attain it.

Baba Arjoondas

Such a holy man was present, some years ago, at the great Kumbha-fair at Allahabad. These fairs are held every twelve years at such centres of Hindu culture as Haridwar, near the source of the Ganges, or Allahabad at the junction of the Jamuna and the Ganges, or Nasik on the Godavari, and are like great religious congresses, where the holy mendicants and devotees of India periodically assemble, and spend a few weeks, cultivating mutual acquaintances and exchanging spiritual offices with one another. Baba Arjoondas, one of the most renowned of the Hindu saints of our day, was present at the Kumbha of 1894-95. One day a friend of mine (who also had been on a visit to this fair) saw him crying on the roadside, saying that he had been thrashed by a policeman. This very much upset my friend. Such an outrage was unthinkable even in India, and he begged Arjoondas to point out to him the man who had committed this cowardly sacrilege. They both walked along the road for some time, the Baba crying all the while, until a policeman was found. My friend now asked Baba Arjoondas, if this was the offending constable. At this the Baba seemed to come back to himself, and said,—"the policemen beat 'not this me' but 'another me'.

Those who have seen him know how he lives in a perpetual consciousness of the Universal. He is a devotee of Rama, one of the incarnations of Vishnu or the Supreme Lord, according to the sacred traditions of the Hindus, and he sees his Rama in every human being. He once came to Calcutta. It was during the hot summer days. A friend of mine went to see him. The day was very sultry and my friend was literally bathed in perspiration as he walked up the stairs of the house where Arjoondas was staying. Immediately he saw my friend, Baba Arjoondas came up to him, and commenced actually to adore him, after the manner of the Hindus, by devoutly moving the right palm before his face and all the time repeating to himself his favourite formula—"O ! my darling

Rama ! O ! my darling Rama !" This devout greeting over, the Baba took up a fan and for full one hour and a quarter fanned my friend with the loving tenderness with which the mother fans the tired and perspiring limbs of her dearly beloved son. And all this time he was explaining the methods and disciplines of *bhakti-yoga* or union with God through love and faith, citing copious texts not only from ancient Sanskrit scriptures but also from the vernacular devotional literature of Upper India. To the spiritual vision of this devout Hindu, there is really no such thing as mere man. In every human he realises his Rama, the incarnation of the Supreme Lord, according to the Hindu Vaishnavas. Indeed, Baba Arjoondas seeks to reach out to the loftiest conception of humanity through his beloved Rama, even as the truly illumined Christian tries to reach through his beloved Christ ; though perhaps the emotional and spiritual moods of the Hindu are deeper and more varied than those of the Christian.

Baba Arjoondas can see no evil in any man, not even in those who are diametrically opposed, in their life and habits, to himself. Another friend of mine was once walking along a street of Calcutta with Arjoondas, and seeing a European on the way, the Baba wanted to know who he was. My friend, to test the universality of the Baba's love and humanity, spoke very deprecatingly of the European, saying that he was a *mlechha*—an unclean person, who had no holiness in him and who ate and drank everything with everybody. At this Baba Arjoondas enthusiastically exclaimed, his face beaming with loving admiration —"what great love have they, what great love! They eat and drink with everybody, oh my darling Rama!—what great love is here!" Yet Baba Arjoondas, and the type he represents, would be described as a heathen and an idolater by many a European observer, both lay and missionary, though those who have come in contact with the Baba declare that there is a greater spirituality and a deeper and more living God-consciousness in the so-called idolatry of this Vaishnava devotee than is found in all the aggressive and dogmatic missionary religions of the world that claim the exclusive privilege of worshipping the One True God in spirit and in truth.

Another Holy Man

Hindu saints and devotees cultivate their sympathetic imagination not only in regard to men but equally also in regard to the lower animals and even in regard to vegetables. All that have sentience are included in the term *jeeva*. Men and animals and vegetables are all *jeeva* in

Sanskrit. And love of the *jeeva* is a universal Hindu ideal. In seeking to realise it, our saints and devotees always cultivate what may be called a kind of vicarious identity with all these. Their love of men is thus of the same class as their love of self. Their love of animals and vegetables is again of the same class as their love of men. There is thus almost an element of personal romance in their love of nature, as well as in their love of men. Their enjoyment of the beauty of birds and beasts and of flowers and plants has therefore more than mere a æsthetic reference, it is supremely spiritual. They not only love but actually lose themselves sometimes in both animals and vegetables as much as they do in other humans like themselves. Such a holy man was living, many years ago, at Kalighat, in southern Calcutta. The capacity for vicarious suffering and enjoyment had been very exceptionally developed, even for a Hindu devotee, in this saintly man. Many a time, while walking along the streets of this modern suburb, if he happened to see any poor woman, sitting by the roadside or in her hut or shop nursing her baby, this holy man would lose all consciousness of his individuality in the suckling baby, and going to its mother would gently push it aside, and placing his hoary head on her lap, would commence to behave with her as if she was his own mother and he her baby boy. The same transfiguration happend also, occasionally in regard to the other sacred emotions. But the peculiarity of this type of spirituality was his almost complete identification even with the animal and the vegetable kingdoms. One day stray bull entered his garden and commenced to eat up his flowers and plants. Moved by love for the vegetables, he rushed out stick in hand, to drive the intruder away. But when he went near it, and saw how the bull was enjoying its excellent feast, he stood dumb and motionless, tears flowing from his eyes. On the one hand, he felt in his own self the intense pain of the vegetables at the loss of their tender leaves and shoots ; on the other hand, he simultaneously felt also the deep satisfaction of the bull in his own soul. And torn between these two conflicting emotions, he did not know what to do. The conflict of emotions became almost unbearable to him, and as he explained to a devoted visitor, torn by it his heart cried out, "Oh God ! Why should there be this cruel antagonism in Thy creation, so that the happiness and enjoyment of one class or individual can only be secured through the misery and deprivation of another !"

An Actual Supperman

They talk and write, as you know, a lot of

fanciful nonsense in Europe of the coming superman. Judging from the picture drawn of him by some at least of your writers, this superman seems to me to mean only a superior animal. When you come however to India, my child, you will see what this superman truly is. He belongs to the class of which I have been speaking here. We do not call them supermen. In our language and literature they are called—*jeevanmookta*, which literally means, emancipated-in-life. They are freed from all bondage, physical, intellectual and moral, even in this life. Not that the body absolutely ceases to be subject to physical laws and conditions, or that the intellect or the conscience ceases to work naturally ; but only this that the *jeevanmookta* are able to transcend, at their will, the mental and moral limitations, which our senses and our intellect impose upon us. They are able, it is said, to transcend outer physical limitations as well.

Pandit Bijay Krishna Goswami

I have myself had the supreme good fortune of sitting at the feet of a holy man, Pandit Bijay Krishna Goswami, who had actually attained this supreme spiritual ideal. He was a Bengalee. In early youth he had fallen in with the movement of social and religious freedom in India, known as the Brahmo Samaj. Along with Maharshi Debendra Nath Tagore and Brahmananda Keshub Chunder Sen, Bijay Krishna also held the highest position among the pioneers of this reform movement. In later life he fully attained the high spiritual state described as ***Brahma-nirvana*** in our books. He was a living superman, a true example of *jeevanmookta.*

We read in the Upanishads that the devotee who has seen the Supreme, has had "all the knots of his heart cut through (*i. e.*, all his self-regarding desires absolutely killed), all his spiritual doubts completely dispelled, and all his *karma* (*i. e.*, the seeds of all possible self-regarding activities in the future, whether here or hereafter) absolutely worn out." This is our ideal of the superman. This is the real thing, which modern fancy has commenced to speak of as "beyond good and evil". Pandit Bijay Krishna Goswami, like his saintly contemporary, Paramhansa Ramakrishna,—a very meagre and imperfect sketch of whom was given out to the English-speaking world some years ago by Professor Max Muller,—had attained this state. Bijay Krishna had killed all conceit of self in him. His spiritual detachment from his body and his senses was complete. In moments of illness he used always to say that it was the body which suffered for its own *karma*—the conscious or unconscious violation of the laws of health,—but these sufferings did not in the least affect his mind and soul. Upon the death of his saintly wife, he wrote to his daughter—"Your mother has gone to the other world. It is not proper to grieve for her, but rather rejoice." The thin partition that divided the here from the hereafter had no existence in his spiritual vision. When his younger daughter died, though he had been exceedingly fond of her, instead of any depression, those who were about him saw a strange transfiguration in him. It was like Christ's vision of Eliza. Every death in his family seemed indeed to open afresh the portals of the holy spirit-world to his vision. Neither death nor life made any real difference to him. His disciplined and illumined spirit had actually learnt to transcend both time and space. Near or far, presence or absence were the same to him. Neither health nor disease, nor wealth nor poverty, nor adulation nor abuse, nor fame nor shame, made the least little difference to this saintly Bengalee. All religions were the same to him,—the revelations of his God. All sects were the same to him, who claimed no special relations with any. All men were the same to him,—the image of God, the temple of the Deity. In his life and conversation one could see the loftiest and the most transcendental teachings of our ancient scriptures visibly verified. Yet, there was little or nothing of so-called supernaturalism in him. Not that he absolutely disbelieved in the supernatural, but only this, that in the spirit of ancient Hindu seers and sages, he always condemned all signs and wonders as a hindrance to the attainment of the highest love and faith. Many an English-educated Indian, who, in the name of science and reason, had at one time dismissed his national scriptures as fanciful and false, got back the lost faith by coming in contact with this holy man, and by thus seeing these old records verified in his life and character.

Like Baba Arjoondas, Pandit Bijay Krishna Goswami also, inspite of his early modernism and rationalism, had developed a most wonderful sympathetic imagination. To see any keen human suffering was, for him, to have it directly transferred to his own sensations. One wintry morning he was sitting in his usual place in the Brahmo Samaj mission house at Dacca facing the garden beyond which was the public road. All of a sudden he seemed to take ill with a severe fit of shivering. His people did not know what it meant, or what to do. A disciple, however, noticed that his eyes were fixed on a decrepit old beggar seated on the footpath on the other side of the public road, who was shivering in all his bare limbs at the touch of the sharp frosty morning breeze. He at once took the heavy blanket that covered the master's body, and running out to the street, put it round the old beggar. As soon as this was done, the master came back to himself, and all his shivering ceased. It was not the only incident of its kind in the life of this saintly Hindu. The experience was repeated, so far as there is any record, once at Darbhanga in Bihar, and again at Allahabad in the winter of 1894-95 where Bijay Krishna had gone to attend the Kumbha-fair.

The True Indian Prototype

It is these holy men of India, my child, both Hindu and Mahomedan, who furnish us with the right key to the interpretation of Indian life and institutions. They are the genuine products of the soil. They are the finest fruits of our social and religious institutions. In them the highest possibilities of the special thought and culture of our people have been fully brought out. It is these holy men who have, from generation to generation, maintained the essential continuity of our culture while progressively adjusting our socio-religious life and institutions to the changing conditions, both physical and social, of their people. There is no lifeless formalism or hidebound conservatism in these men. Their illumined intellect and absolutely selfless lives enabled them from age to age to initiate social and religious progress without the violent revolts through which the social and religious evolution of Europe has uniformly sought to work itself out. Rising above all personal passions and prejudices and all carnal conflicts between the individualities and particularities of social life and religious opinions, and in every way thus identifying themselves with the universal, they have been able to harmonise order with progress and prevent the growth of the spirit of revolution and anarchy in their community. It is to these men that we owe all the peculiar developments of our social, our moral and our religious life. In Europe the history of socio-ethical evolution has been different from that in India. From status, through the revolt of right, to the highest ideal of duty, in the modern sense of complete and perfect self-realisation by the faithful discharge of the obligations imposed upon the individual by his station in life,—this has been the scheme of socio-ethical evolution in Christendom. In India, owing to the peculiar synthetic genius of the people and the control of the course of social evolution not by rebels and reformers but by its spirit-illumined saints and sages, the scheme of socio-ethical evolution has been directly from status to duty for its own sake. Similarly, the evolution of religion in India has also been fundamentally different from that of Europe. In the earliest stage religion is ethnic, miscalled national by some European students of religious history. Judaism, the tribal religions of Arabia before the birth of Islam, as well as the earliest forms of our own Vedic religion, all belong to this ethnic type. From the ethnic stage, religious evolution, both in Christendom and in Islam, passed through a credal stage to true universalism. The evolution of religion in India somehow skipped over the intermediate stage of credalism. Hinduism has never been a credal religion. The Buddhistic protest did develop a creed and, as it seems to me, on account of this very credal character, the spirit of Hinduism threw out Buddhism, as every strong and healthy organism throws out a foreign body that accidentally enters it. And these peculiarties of our history and progress are, as it seems to me, entirely due to the controlling influence exercised over the course of our socio-religious evolution by successive generations of our holy men.

They are the true prototypes of Indian humanity. A tree must not only be judged by its fruit but should also be interpreted by it. The child should be interpreted by the man, and not the man by the child. The meaning of the individuals belonging to a type must be sought for and found in its prototype. It is therefore that if you really desire to correctly understand and truly appreciate our life and culture, you must try my child, first and foremost of all, to study, to love and thus to understand the holy men of India.

Characteristics of the Indian Ideal

Absolute self-detachment and a unique and lofty idealism are the main characteristics of these holy men. These are the essential elements of the true spiritual life, as we in India have always understood it. And it is here in this detatchment and idealism that you must seek the right key to the correct interpretation of all apparent perplexities of our social institutions and religious life. It is on account of this detachment and this idealism that a community controlled by a most rigid system of castes rarely suffered from class-war or developed any violent spirit of mutual jealousy or recrimination among its members until we commenced very recently to improve and reform it by the individualistic, capitalistic and competitive class-distinctions of the imported socio-political ideals of modern European civilisation.

In our old caste-life, there was no conscious

conceit of superiority in the so-called higher and, therefore, no rankling sense of inferiority in the so-called lower castes, and this was due to the spirit of detachment that has stood at the back, not always of our conscious but certainly of our sub-conscious life. And we should always remember that the elements of our sub-conscious life furnish far stronger proofs of our real character than the conventionalities and artificialities that constitute so large a portion of what we call our conscious life.

And if our spirit of detachment saved our society from the ugly rivalries of the competetive class-distinctions of modern Europe, our idealism always helped us to transcend all forms of social inequalities, due to convention or culture, and realise the Divine as much in the Brahmin as in the Pariah.

Dharma—The Basis Of Our Civilisation

These two fundamental characteristics of our culture,—detachment and idealism—have been combined into an organic whole, in our conception of *dharma*, loosely rendered by the English word religion. Strictly speaking, the concept is untranslatable. There is no doubt some slight affinity between the radical meaning of the two words: *dharma* is derived from Sanskrit *dhri* to hold, and religion from Latin *ligare* to bind.

Dharma is that which holds together the different elements of a thing and thus combines them into one organic whole. Religion is that which binds men together. The conception of religion is thus exclusively human and social ; that of *dharma* is cosmic and universal. The elements have no religion. We can never speak of the religion of fire, or water, or ether or air. But we always speak in Sanskrit, and all the Sanskrit-derived vernaculars of India, of the *dharma* of these elements. Heat is thus the *dharma* of fire, coolness of water, sound of ether, motion of air. Everything in creation has its *dharma*. The most correct rendering of our *dharma* is to be found in your word Law—with a capital "L". It is Law in the specific Emersonian sense,—the Law of Being. And as every object, whether animate or inanimate, whether vegetable, animal or human---has its own law of being, so we can reasonably use the word *dharma* in regard to them all.

This Law or Law of Being is not, however, imposed upon objects from without, but grows from within, through the general course of their history and evolution. It is what in the philosophy of evolution, they call the Regulative Idea. It is something constitutional. And as the constitutions of different things differ, so this *dharma* also organises and expresses itself differently in different objects. As there are constitutional differences between one individual human and another, so the *dharma* of one man cannot truly be the *dharma* of another. It is something essentially specific and personal. The law and course of ethical and spiritual evolution in one person cannot, therefore, be necessarily the same as that of another. What is good for one, may not therefore be good for another. There must consequently be great diversities of both faiths and cultures in the community, owing to fundamental constitutional differences between the individuals composing it. Hinduism has always recognised this fact. It is, therefore, not one religion, like Christianity or Islam, but a federation of many cults and cultures. The Hindu society is also, for the same reason, not a homogeneous unit but rather a highly developed organic whole which seeks to realise its essential unity not by denying but openly accepting and harmonising in the totality of its life, the endless diversities of its component organisms. Like the Hindu religion, the Hindu society is also not a homogeneous unit but a federation of many units. The freedom and integrity of the parts inside the unity of the whole, is the very soul and essence of the federal idea. And in no religion or society that I know of, has this organic federal ideal been sought to be so fully realised as in the Hindu religion and the Hindu society. And because of this wonderful combination of isolation and association, of freedom and federation, in the very constitution of our society and religion, you find that in a country inhabited by so many races, racial antagonism has scarcely been known; and among a people divided into so many sects and cults never had the stake or the rack been set up for the spiritual benefit of the heretic. The word of Indian Evolution is *Dharma*; the word of European Evolution is Right. And these two words seem, to my mind, to completely sum up the fundamental difference between India and Europe. *Dharma* is the law of renunciation, Right is the law of. resistance. *Dharma* demands self-abnegation, Right self-assertion. *Dharma* develops collectivism, Right individualism. *Dharma* works for synthesis, Right lives and grows in antithesis. *Dharma* is the soul of order, Right the parent of revolution. To understand India we must seize the conception of *Dharma*. To understand Europe we must seize the principle of Right. How then, can the generalisations of European experience, gathered under the Law of Right, help one to interpret the character and culture of India, trained in the ideal of *Dharma*? India, my child, must therefore interpret herself.

LETTER II

THE NAME AND THE THING

Personal and Prefatory

I am very glad, indeed, that you liked my last letter. I was rather afraid that you would find it tediously long, and, in places, rather dry and abstruse. Of course, I could not help it. I have had to clear the ground, and state the reasons why India has not yet been understood by Europe. The fact that, inspite of its length and abstruseness, you found it, as you say, so "entrancingly" interesting, proves, however, not the quality of my exposition, but only the strength of your love for India. I am exceedingly gratified to find this fresh proof of your romantic admiration for our country and culture. It is the surest of all assurances that sooner or later you will be able to understand us such as but few foreigners have as yet been able to do.

The True Interpreter

You want me to undertake the work of interpreting India to the modern world. You know not, my child, what you are asking for. I do not possess, as my friends know, any excess of humility in my composition. But with all my conceit, I dare not claim the intellectual and spiritual qualifications necessary in a true interpreter of India. My vision of India is yet rather dim and hazy. It specially lacks that definiteness of details so essential to every faithful and illuminating picture. I am only feeling after her. Not to speak of myself, I know only two or three persons, among all our most intelligent and highly educated people, who have had the fullest equipment for this work. Some may claim wide scholarship, the fruit of laborious study and research, but lack that consuming passion for their country and culture, without which the soul of things can never be seized. Others may have a kind of native love for their own land and people but lack large scholarship and deep insight. The interpreter must be absolutely possessed by the spirit of the thing he seeks to interpret. But can we, of the present generation in India, claim this possession ? We are much too completely possessed by the spirit of modern Europe, to be effectually seized by the real spirit of India. We are the fruits of a hybrid education that has produced a kind of intellectual and spiritual atavism in us. This education has, on the one hand, divorced our mind and spirit from the deeper realities of the life and thought of our own country, without, on the other hand, placing us in any living and real relations even with the life and thought of Europe. We scarcely understand Europe, however much we may ape her ways. We cannot understand India, however much we may swear aloud by her name. How then shall we be able to interpret her ?

The Reformer and The Reactionary

Broadly speaking, we, the so-called modern-educated classes of India, stand divided into two opposite camps. Some are reformers, some are reactionaries. But neither of these have, to my mind, any real and correct appreciation of their own country and culture. The reformer, applying the untested canons of imported European enlightenment to the examination of the surface values of Indian life and institutions, sees signs of almost universal degradation and decadence about him. India may have been great and noble, wise and strong, pious and pure, at one time. But now she is mean and ignoble, ignorant and weak, godless and vicious. This is the ordinary reformer's estimate of his own country and culture. You might as legitimately go to him for a correct understanding of Indian life and institutions as you might for instance, seek the Mahomedan Moulavi for a faithful and illuminating inter-pretation of Hindu ritualism or the Christian Trinity. The standard of judgment which the reformer applies to the examination of his own culture, in passing his cruel verdict on it, is derived neither from the rational generalisation of the course of history and evolution in India itself, nor even from those of universal history and culture, but from the crude conclusions of European empiricism. European society is democratic, the Indian patriarchal. The latter is, therefore, necessarily lower than the former. There is considerable latitude of social intercourse in Europe, in India it is hedged in by multitudinous restrictions of sex and caste. India is, therefore, fundamentally inferior to Europe in the matter of social progress. In Europe the masses are, to a large extent, literate and therefore enducated. In India they are illiterate and necessarily uneducated and unintelligent. This is the general way in which the reformer examines and judges India. Judging them in the light of the history and achievements of Europe, he constantly condemns his own country and culture, and with the relentless pity of the missionary propagandist seeks to ruthlessly improve them more or less after these alien ideals.

The reactionary, from a different motive, and pursuing quite an opposite method, also applies unconsciously the standards of Europe, not to abolish but rather to revive and re-establish the social and religious institutions of his country. In religion, the reactionary is setting up for the Indian scriptures the same claims to infallibility and absolutism, that credal systems like Christianity or Islam popularly claim for the Bible or the Koran. He forgets that neither verbal infallibility nor any exclusive and absolute authority had ever been vested in the religious scriptures of Hinduism. In sociology, the reactionary tries to revive the relaxing rigidities of the Indian caste-system in the spirit of the class domination of Europe ; and thereby he ignores the patent fact that the genius of the Indian caste-system never tolerated this spirit of domination in the so-called higher, and consequently, rarely evoked any spirit of envious revolt in the so-called lower castes. Conceit of superiority has been uniformly condemned in the higher castes ; while, the almost absolute autonomy enjoyed by the different castes in regard to all matters concerning their caste-life, and the sense of mutual interdependence cultivated in all the castes, both higher and lower, as limbs and organs of a great organic whole,—left, indeed, but little room for the growth of such conceits.

The reactionary is thus as much under the

spell of European ideas and ideals as the reformer. The only difference between them is that while the reformer is trying to consciously control and regulate his social evolution after the manner of Europe, the reactionary is unconscious of the domination of these alien ideas. The strange psychological affinity between these two rival camps will be clearly realised when we remember that there are only two ways of intellectual and spiritual appropriation. One is the way of love, the other of hatred ; for love and hatred both—and hatred, perhaps, even more than love,—help us to be possessed by the thing we love or hate. In love as well as in hatred there is deep concentration of the mind on the object of our emotion. And we always unconsciously become that which we constantly think of. The reformer becomes a convert by his love, the reactionary by his hatred, to European ideals and institutions.

Both the reformer and the reactionary are thus found, at the final analysis, to be equally inspired, the one consciously, and the other unconsciously, by the spirit of Europe. Both have, more or less, imbibed the European temperament. Both are, though in different ways, emphatically objective and materialistic. The one is dominated by individualistic ethicism, the other by effete formalism ; and both these equally lack that true inwardness which is characteristic of the thought and culture of India. The one revels in the unrealities of subjective abstractions ; the other in the unrealities of effete and ununderstood rituals. The reformer by his unillumined and empirical criticism of our life and institutions strengthens the forces of reaction in the country ; while the reactionary by the infidel tenacity with which he is seeking to hold on to the lifeless and decadent forms of our social and religious life, lends strength and vitality to the reformer's revolt. And in their mutual wranglings and recriminations, the perception of the true Soul of India is lost. You will find the real truth about India in the presentation of neither of these two classes. It lies really in the traditional Middle Path of the sage and the philosopher. I am only a humble enquirer, my child, seeking light and guidance into that Holy Path. How can I dare to pose as a guide to others ?

But though I dare not accept the holy office of the interpreter of India, I may well, and quite legitimately, undertake to study and understand her. It is, indeed, not only the high privilege, but a distinct duty, of even the least of her children, to try to understand her through reverent and diligent study and investigation. This much, my child, I can, and will do for you : and if it should in any way help you to a better and deeper understanding and appreciation of our culture and civilisation than what you have now, I shall thankfully consider all my labours more than amply repaid.

India As Seen By The Stranger

To begin, then, from the very name of India, we have to remember that this name was given her not by her own children but by the strangers within her gate. We never called her either India or Hindoostan. We knew her of old by quite a different name.

The strangers came to us, in the early days of our history, by our north-western land-route. This is the way that the Babylonians and the Assyrians, the Persians, and later the Greeks also came to us. In seeking to do so they had to cross a great river. Our own native name for that great river was Sindhu. It is still known among us by that ancient name. The sibilant "S" of our Sindhu became, however, the aspirant "H" in the tongue of the Babylonians and the Persians. Our Sindhu became their Hindu. You would do well to remember that the original reference to this word Hindu was not to our religion, but simply to one of our great rivers. The Hindu of the Babylonians and the Persians became the Indus of the Greeks and the Romans. The land of the Indus became India.

India A Mere Geographical Expression

In its origin and history India is thus truly and really what the present-day European, either from ignorance or pride, is so anxious to prove. It is undoubtedly a mere geographical expression. It indicates simply a distinctive geographical feature of the country. In fact, the geographical boundaries of this land are so peculiar and prominent, that we cannot blame the stranger if he be so profoundly impressed by them as to entirely forget or ignore its more fundamental and significant features. The Himalayas on the north, and the sea on the south, as well as practically also towards the east and the west of the Peninsula, demarcate this land from the rest of the Asiatic continent. Both these are most prominent physical features of the country. Such boundaries are scarcely found anywhere in our known world, except in relation to what we call continents. The physical isolation of India is really continental. So also is the immense extent of her territory. She has the largest surface area of any country in the world,—China, Russia and the United States excepted. The total area of India is nearly one-third of that of the continent of Europe. It is nearly fourteen times as large as Great Britain, and over ten times the size of the entire British Isles. It is a good deal over five times the area of Austria-

Hungary, and more than six times that of either France or Germany. So immense a tract of territory, covering so many latitudes and longitudes, must naturally have quite a variety of physical and physiographical features also. It is a land of many altitudes and many climates. In some places you will find the suffocating heat of the tropics, in others the more pleasant and equable temperature of the true temperate zones ; while there are places in India where you may find as much snow and frost in the winter months, as the heart of the most homesick Englishman or Scotchman may be pining for. There are provinces in India where we have the highest records of the world's rainfall, as in the Khasi Hills ; while in some other places as Sind, there is hardly any rainfall from year's end to year's end. With such diversities of physical and physiographical conditions and characters, it is only natural that India should have an equally large variety of both flora and fauna. Both in its physical features, and in the wealth and variety of its vegetable and animal kingdoms, this extensive tract of territory is truly continental. It is equally large and diversified in its human populations also. The total strength of our population counts one-fifth of the whole human race. We have the largest population of any country in the world, with the exception of the Chinese Empire. We are over ten times as many as the English and the Welsh combined, nine times as many as the French, six times as many as the Germans, four times as many as the Americans and quite three times as many as the Russians. In this huge mass of humanity almost all the great racial varieties of mankind are more or less represented. The main body of the population is perhaps of Aryan origin, though there has been considerable admixture with other races, during the many thousand years that have elapsed since the Aryans first settled in this country. The Dravidians dominate the populations of the southern part of the Peninsula, while there is an unmistakable Mongolian element in the populations of the north-eastern provinces. There is an equally strong Negroid element among the dark aboriginal races ; while the Semitic blood dominates a very large percentage of that higher section of the Moslem community in India, who, like the Normans in England, came over to us with the Mahomedan conquest. This teeming population, composed of different original racialities, speak many languages, profess many faiths, and obey many social and sacerdotal laws and customs. And all these bewildering diversities of racial origin, as well as of languages and literatures, and cults and customs, combine to strengthen the first impression produced by the physical characteristics of the land upon the uninitiated stranger, namely, that it is not a country but a continent.

The Popular Anglo-Indian View

This is, really, the most popular and prevailing view of India in Europe and America. The European or the American visitor to India comes to us with this strong prepossession, and all his outer experience of our country and people, instead of dissipating, helps, on the contrary, to confirm and strengthen this view. He cannot discover any fundamental principle of unity at the back of these bewildering diversities, except perhaps that new administrative, political, social and economic unity which the establishment of the British Empire has been working in our own time. Every Anglo-Indian publicist assiduously proclaims that India is not a country but a collection of countries, which have as little or as much in common with one another, either in race or history, as the German, the French, the Dutch, the Russian, the Italian, the English and the Spaniard in Europe have between them. It would be as correct, they declare, to view Europe as one country and the different nations of the great continent as one nation or people as it would be to regard India as one land, and the so-called Indians as one people. In fact, there is no such thing as an Indian ; there are the Bengalees, the Mahrattas, the Tamilians, the Telegus, the Shiks, the Gurkhas,—Hindus, Mahomedans, Jains and Buddhists—but really no Indians ; in any case, there never was such an animal as an Indian, until the British rulers of the country commenced so generously to manufacture him with the help of their schools and their colleges, their courts and their camps, their law and their administration, and their free press and open platform. This is also the orthodox official view of India, that finds repeated utterance and authoritative exposition from responsible Anglo-Indian rulers and prominent British politicians. Nor can it be denied that there is a very large element,—not of truth, but surely of strong plausibility—in this popular and orthodox official view. The fact of the matter really is, that as long as you look upon our country as "India, or the Land of the Indus"—you will get no closer and truer view of it than what the foreign officials and students have been able to do.

India As Known To Her Own Children

But while the stranger called her India, or the Land of the Indus, thereby emphasising only her strange physical features, her own children, from of old, have known and loved her by another name. We never called her India. Long before the Greek invasion and even before the Babylonians and Assyrians came in any sort of close contact with us, we had given this name to our country. That name is Bharatavarsha. To clearly understand and grasp the nature and reality of the fundamental unity in which all our divergent and even apparently conflicting usuages and customs, cults and cultures, our racialities and provincialities, have almost from the very beginning of our history been rationally reconciled, you must try to realise the deep significance of this old and native name of the land which the foreigner has so long called and known as India.

Meaning Of Geographical Names

Geographical names belong to three classes : some have a mere physical origin and reference, some have an ethnic or tribal origin, and some, much fewer in number, have what may be called a personal and historic origin and reference. Names like the Transvaal, derived from the river Vaal, and India, from the river Indus, belong to the first class. Aryavarta, the old name of what is now known as Upper India, derived from the Aryas or Aryans who settled there, and England from the Angels, belong to the second or the ethnic group. Rome from Romulus, and Bharatavarsha from Bharata,—

these belong to the third and historic group of geographical names. And wherever a country is commenced to be called after some great historic personage, especially some great king or potentate, whether real or legendary, there necessarily lies at the back of it a distinct historic or national consciousness. Rome did not connote any geographical features of the city or principality that received this name, nor any tribality of its people, nor even any religious unity or affinity that might have existed among them, but predominantly, and even exclusively, an individual civic or national entity. It had, of course, like all other places under human habitation, its physicalities and its tribalities, its socialities and its religiosïties ; but the particular name by which it came to be known among men, referred to none of these, but prominently and almost exclusively, to what may be called its civic unity or national individuality. Her name itself was the most conclusive proof that Rome was not a mere geographical entity, or the habitat of a particular tribe or groups of tribes, but had developed a distinct national consciousness.

The Meaning Of Bharatavarsha

Those who so persistently deny any fundamental historic unity or any real national individuality to our land and our people, either do not know, or do not remember the fact that we never called our country by the alien name of India or even by that of Hindoostan. Our own name was, and is still today, among the Aryan populations of the country, Bharatavarsha. And Bharatavarsha is not a physical name like India or the Transvaal, nor even a tribal or ethnic name like England or Aryavarta, but a distinct and unmistakable historic name like Rome. It is derived from Bharata. This Bharata is as much a historic personage as Romulus. Strictly speaking, both Bharata and Romulus are more legendary than perhaps historical. But the profound significance of the name which they gave to these two great countries of the ancient world, is by no means affected by their legendary or even mythical character. India may not be one country but a collection of countries confined within certain prominent physical boundaries. It may be peopled by many races, speaking many languages, professing many religions and owning many cultures. But those who gave it one common name must have realised some fundamental unity at the back of all these endless diversities. Men never call any collection of things of divergent characters or properties by one single name, unless they are able to seize some prominent and undeniable principle of unity in them. Those who gave the name of

Bharatavarsha to India must have done so. And the unity that they seized behind the diversities of the life of their country was not a mere physical or even a mere tribal or ethnic unity, like that which is indicated by such geographical names as India or Aryavarta ; but was an essentially historic or national unity as is connoted by the name Rome. India was then, as it is now, divided into many provinces, inhabited by many peoples, with their peculiar cultures and characteristics, represented many faiths and cults, and had many languages and literatures. And yet all these endless diversities notwithstanding, it was called by one common name. And this fact conclusively proves the presence of some undeniable principle of historic or national unity in the consciousness of the people or peoples who lived in this land even in those early days.

The Character of Indian Unity

What then was the real character of this Indian unity ? Bharata was, like Romulus, a king. He is a Vedic personage. Though described as the lord and master of the "world with all the seas," it cannot be held that he was the real ruler of all the territories that received his name and came to be called his "*varsha.*" The limit of Bharatavarsha extended in those days even much further than the present limits of India. Balk, called in our ancient books Balhik, and Kandahar, our old Gandhar, were among its north-western provinces. Towards the east, Bharatavarsha extended as far as the very confines of the Chinese Empire. It is incredible that in those early days, this extensive tract was subject to one single king or emperor. In fact, such political sovereignty or administrative centralisation as would be implied by any hypothesis of this character, was foreign to the genius of the Aryan people of India. Even at the time of the Mahabharata, which was much later than that of this Bharata, from whom our land derived its significant name, it was not in any sense a political and administrative unit like the present British Empire in India. The epithets applied to king Bharata are also quite impartially applied to many other great kings who figured at the great Bharata war. Every powerful monarch is described in our old books as lord and master of the whole world. Bharata was undoubtedly a great king. He is described as a *rajachakravarti*, very loosely rendered into English sometimes by the word emperor. But neither Bharata, nor indeed any of the great monarchs spoken of in the old books, was an emperor in the modern sense. Modern empires have grown through conquests and appropriations of the lands of other sovereigns. But we scarcely find any evidence of such earth-hunger in our old kings and warriors. Kings no doubt fought with one another : but it was very rarely indeed that the victor appropriated to himself the territories of the vanquished. The usual practice, on the contrary, was to place some son or relation of the defeated monarch upon his throne, even where, for any reason, the vanquished, if still living, could not be placed back into his old position and authority. The Hindu *rajachakravarti* was therefore not an emperor, as he is known in Europe, but was simply the nominal head of a federation of kingdoms and principalities. Indeed, the literal meaning of the term is not emperor, but only a king "established at the centre of a circle of kings." King Bharata was a great prince of this order. As a *rajachakravarti*, his political position in the land was not that of the administrative head of any large and centralised government, but only that of the recognised and respected centre and symbol of a confederation of brother princes. This was the general character of all our great princes in the old days. And this being so it is not possible to hold that the unity indicated by the name Bharatavarsha was, in any way, either a political or administrative unity. Neither was it a religious or sacerdotal unity. Like Krishna or Buddha, Christ or Mahomed, this Bharata was not the founder or centre of any creed or cult. He was not even the promulgator of any social or sacerdotal code. Indeed, there were in the days, when our land first received this name of Bharatavarsha, almost as many sects and schools of religion in this country as there are now. The unity that this name Bharatavarsha indicated, was thus not a religious unity either. In the presence of many races and cultures in India, even in those early days, convincing evidence of which is supplied by all our old books, it is equally impossible that this unity should have been a mere racial unity. What, then, is the character of the unity which lies at the back of this name Bharatavarsha, by which we have called and known our country from almost the very beginning of our history ?

The unity of India was, thus neither racial nor religious, nor political nor administrative. It was a peculiar type of unity, which may, perhaps be best described as cultural. Bharata stood before the multitudinous peoples that inhabited the territories that took his name, as the representative of a great civilisation and culture. Bharata was, as I have said, a Vedic character. It is not at all likely that at the early period of our history when our continent received this name of Bharatvarsha, the Aryan settlers had actually spread themselves over the whole land. Even at the time of the Mahabharata, there were extensive tracts not yet brought within the control of the Aryans. But still, it can scarcely be doubted that from a much earlier period of the history of this land, the Aryan civilisation had commenced to profoundly influence and visibly dominate it from end to end. And it was as the representative and symbol of this dominating culture, that Bharata gave his name to this great continent, though it was divided then as now into many provinces and principalities, inhabited by many races, speaking many dialects, professing many religions and obeying different laws and customs.

Aryan Expansion in India

What I have called the cultural character of Indian unity, is due partly to the peculiar genius of the Indo-Aryan, and partly to the very peculiar methods by which the Aryan settlers of India spread themselves over the whole of this continent, quietly absorbing the numerous races and cultures of the land into their own body. These methods are practically unknown in the other parts of the world. The methods of social expansion known to history, in the other parts of the world, are either through religious proseletyzation, or through political conquests and more often, perhaps, through a combination of the two. Both the Christian and the Moslem communities of the world grew thiswise. It is the common method of social expansion in all credal religions. As we find it in the history of Christianity or Islam, so we find it in the history of Buddhistic expansion also. The mere acceptance of the Buddhist or the Christian or the Moslem creed, makes a person at once a member of the Buddhist, the Christian or the Mahomedan community. This has been one method of social expansion. The other method is political. It is the method of conquest. In this method, sometimes the conquering people spread themselves over the conquered country, and slowly assimilate the conquered races into their own body, or, if the disparity in culture between the two be too wide for such assimilation, the latter are driven out and become gradually extinct as has happned in our own age to the American Indians and the Australian aborigines. Sometimes it so happnes also, as we found in the case of the Norman conquerors of England, that it is the conquered, who, possessed with larger virility, slowly assimilate the conquerors into their own body, and thus develop a new and a composite nation, which, however, gradually attains a practically homogeneous character, especially if the process of assimilation be helped by a common credal religion owned and practised by both the component communities.

The expansion of the Aryan society in India followed neither of these two usual methods known to history. The Aryan religion was never credal. Buddhism is no doubt a credal religion, and is of Indo-Aryan origin. But though what may be called Buddhist Imperialism, under the great Asoka, consolidated to a very large extent the fundamental unity of India, Buddhism as a creed had no perceptible influence in this work. In any case, Buddhism did not create the ancient unity of India. The name Bharatavarsha is older than Buddhism, and consequently the unity that was seized by those who gave to our continent this significant historic name, was in no sense a credal religious unity. Nor was it a political unity, as I have already said, due to extensive political conquests and the gradual absorption of the conquered peoples by the conquering community. The early Aryan settlers did no doubt at one time fight and conquer the aboriginal races of northern India. That was a necessity of the situation in which they first found themselves. But the peculiarly peaceful and humanitarian spirit of their culture soon put a stop to these barbarian methods. The Aryan expansion over the greater part of India, and more particularly among the civilised Dravidian peoples of the South, was effected by other and infinitely more civilised and even spiritual means.

The Nature of the Old Aryan Propaganda

Hinduism, as the religion of the Indo-Aryan is popularly called, has never been a missionary religion like Buddhism or Christianity or Islam. These so-called missionary religions are credal, and, therefore, can easily propagate themselves by the prevailing missionary method of mere preaching. These missionary religions have a very prominent intellectual emphasis, and are, therefore, essentially instructive in their methods of propagation. Of course, every religion has its own special disciplines and constructive spiritual rituals. But in the so-called missionary religions, intellectual instructions must precede the real constructive and spiritual disciplines. In all these credal religions, the acceptance of their special dogmas is an absolute condition precedent to the initiation into their truly spiritual disciplines, because these latter have always to work upon the former. The acceptance of the Christian dogmas of the Incarnation and the Trinity is absolutely needed for the pursuit of the inner spiritual disciplines of Christianity.

In all inner spiritual cultures, suggestion and imagination play a very vital part. This suggestion comes in all the credal religions from their particular creeds. These creeds must, therefore, be accepted and fully believed in by those who are to be initiated into the deeper life and culture of these credal religions. In Hinduism, however, owing to its non-credal character, the method has always been predominantly constructive. The true Hindu teacher never asks for any declaration of creed from his pupil, nor even imposes his own, or indeed any sort of intellectual opinions upon him. He does not seek to forcibly shake or destroy the ideas and faiths that the disciple may have imbibed, either from his society or from his parents or previous teachers. Our faiths, he knows, are the result of our inner temperament and outer education and experiences. Real change of faith is, therefore, impossible without a change in this temperament, brought about through a long course of psychophysical, intellectual and ethical disciplines, and the replacement of the old prepossessions by new ones created through a new and different order of experience. When this is done, the legitimate opinions and faiths proper and natural to the disciple's inner intellectual and spiritual state, grow of themselves. Faiths and opinions that grow thuswise have a vitality and truth which no creeds, however natural or healthy these may be, can have, when imposed from the outside through the force of supernatural authority or formal logic. What the true Hindu teacher does, even in our own day, for the propagation of his cult or faith, the ancient Aryan settlers of India did for the promulgation of their special culture among the multitudinous peoples of this continent. They propagated their superior culture, not by the popular missionary methods of preaching and proseletyzation, but through the introduction of their socio-ethical arrangements and disciplines among their non-Aryan neighbours. And they did so by the promulgation of their special social economy.

Varnashaama-Dharma or the Caste-and-Order Law

This social economy is summed up by what is called *Varnashrama-dharma* (the caste-and-order law) in Sanskrit. The castes are, as you know, four in number. They are :—(i) the Brahmins, (ii) the Kshatriyas, (iii) the Vaisyas, and (iv) the Sudras. The first three castes, who alone belonged to the Aryan communion, represnt the three great functions of the social organism, namely, (i) the intellectual and the spiritual, (ii) the administrative and the military and (iii) the economic and the industrial. These are universal social functions. In every society we have people who discharge these three fundamental functions of the social life. The Sudra did not originally belong to the Aryan communion. He was perhaps originally either a captive of war, who according to universal ancient custom, was reduced to the status of the domestic or agricultural labourer in the victorious community ; or, was possibly a member of a very low and primitive tribe or race, absolutely unfitted, both intellectually and morally, to undertake any of the first three functions of the social organism in the more advanced Aryan community.

This caste-system, more or less universal in some shape or other in all old-world civilisations, was, however, joined in India to another, and a supremely significant law and order, known as the *ashrama*, which literally mean stages or stations of life. Society was divided into the above four caste divisions. Individual life was divided into these four *ashrama*-s or stations or stages. Distinctions based upon fundamental social functions, however universal and even necessary for the preservation and development of the collective life of the society, have an inevitable tendency to breed pride in those who are called upon to discharge the superior functions, and envy in those who have to fill the lower places. Division of social functions, especially in the earlier stages of evolution, when the offices have of necessity to be hereditary,—inevitably leads to these moral evils. These divisions cannot be absolutely eliminated from any form of social organisation, however democratic it may be. And a perplexing problem before every healthy society is how to so adjust the relations between the higher offices of society and the individuals who must fill them, that the enjoyment of these offices shall breed no pride of position in them, nor create the conceit of any superior distance between them and the rest of the community. The ancient Indo-Aryan seems to have discovered in this arrangement or order of the *ashrama* or stages, a happy solution of this universal social problem, which even our modern democracies with all their cry of equality and freedom have not yet been able successfully to tackle.

The greatest moral and spiritual danger of the system of caste such as obtained not only in India but in almost every ancient society and culture, in some form or other, lies, as I have said, in the almost inevitable pride of office (and later on also of birth owing to the hereditary character of these offices) which it generates in the so-called higher castes. The only true remedy against this evil is to be found in placing the individual members of the society under some disciplines as will train their minds to habits of more or less complete self-detachment, and thereby prevent them from identifying their individualities with any high social function or office that they may be called upon to fill or discharge. This was, clearly, the object of this law of stages or *ashrama*-s that was joined to the caste-laws of the ancient Aryan community of India. The first of these *ashrama*-s was that of the student or the *brahmachari*. In this stage every individual was absolutely equal to every other individual, whatever the rank or office, that is the caste, of their parents might be. The *brahmachari* in the house of his teacher or *guru* could claim no honour in virtue of his birth or heritage, could earn or own no property, and, whether the son of a prince or of a common soldier, or of an ordinary artisan, had to beg for his daily food from the public, and perform any service, the meanest not excluded, that his *guru* might impose upon him. Here there was absolute equality between one student and another. It was the recognition of the fundamental equality between men as men. He was allowed no vacation such as the modern student has, when he might go home to his parents, and resuming, however temporarily, his place as the son of his father, might thus get into any conceit due to his father's position in the general social order and, thereby, neutralise the effect of the superior disciplines of his order. Here in the *guru's* house, he was a mere individual, without any rights or privileges, equal to every other individual of the community. The next stage was that of the householder. Having finished his tutelage, which generally lasted from the eighth to either the sixteenth or the twenty-fourth year of his life, and sometimes even to a later period,—he entered this stage. Here he became a regular and recognised member of the social body, vested with all the rights and obligations of his particular station in life, whether as king or warior, minister or councillor or priest or teacher, or the producer or seller of commodities. All the inequalities in life came in here, in the householder's stage, and were due entirely to the variety of social functions which different individuals had to discharge. Having thus served society, raised healthy issues, and trained and brought them up in the ways of his caste and position, in the next or the third stage, the individual was encouraged to cultivate the spirit of detachment once more, gradually killing the conceits that might have been bred in him by his accidental place and function as a member of the society. He now retired from active life, and adopted the duties and disciplines of the higher and the contemplative life. And, finally, if he lived long enough, and was able to attain complete self-detachment, he might enter the fourth or the last of these stages or *ashrama*-s, that of the *sannyasin* or the mendicant, when his one aim in life became to absolutely lose all conceit of isolated individuality, and thus identify himself entirely with the Universal.

The ancient Aryan social economy was based upon this *varnashrama*, or caste-and-order scheme. This caste-and-order law sums up the whole soul and spirit of ancient Hindu culture. Through the establishment of this law, the Aryans brought the divergent races and cultures of India within their own fold. And it is here, in this *varnashrama dharma* that we must look for the secret of that strange unity which the name Bharatavarsha implied.

It was comparatively easy for the Indo-Aryan to establish his *varnashrama* law all over this vast continent, because, at certain stages of social evolution, there exists in every society some arrangement or other that wonderfully falls in with the Hindu's system of castes. At this stage there exist in every community individuals or families who, either as priests, or in still lower cultures even as medicinemen, discharge the religious and educational functions of their society, and who, therefore, correspond to the Aryan Brahmins. Similarly there are others who fight and rule, and are therefore akin to the Aryan Kshatriyas. And others again, who are devoted to agriculture or handicrafts and who correspond thus to the Vaishyas of the Aryan economy. In every society there exist, at these earlier stages, another class also, who belong to alien tribes and cultures and being admitted into a dominant and conquering community either as captives of war or in any other way, become mere labourers and slaves. These correspond to the Sudras of the Aryan communion. And owing to this fundamental affinity between the caste-order of the Indo-Aryans and the general social scheme of the non-Aryan communities of India, it became very easy for the former to almost imperceptibly absorb the latter. And they did so by simply putting, so to say, the seal of their own caste-system, upon the already existing social order of their non-Aryan neighbours. This peculiar process of social expansion created absolutely no perceptible disturbance in the communities affected by it. The method was strictly evolutionary, and not revolutionary, as it has generally been in other part of the world.

But the Hindu system of caste did not stand,

as I have already told you, by itself. It was organically bound up with the law of the *ashramas* or stages of life. It is this *ashrama*-law that preserved the humanity of the Hindu in the face of the inequalities created by the system of caste. It was these special disciplines of the *ashramas* which as long as they were faithfully pursued by the so-called higher castes, developed an ideal of spiritual democracy, unknown to the rest of the world ; and it may perhaps be reasonably held that the real cause of the degradations of mediæval Hindu society was not to be found in the system of caste so much, if at all, as in the divorce between the *varnas* and the *ashramas*, between the outer functions and the inequalities of the caste-life, and the inner spiritual ideals and disciplines that were organically connected with these in the earlier periods of our history and culture.

The Ashrama-Law

The Aryans of India did not only put their own caste-seal upon the natural social divisions of their neighbouring non-Aryan communities, which was an easy enough work, but also brought these new social orders under the law and discipline of the *ashramas* or the stages. This was the special contribution of the Aryans of India to the evolution of the non-Aryan communities of the country which they absorbed into themselves. This is how the general character of these non-Aryan communities was fundamentally changed by what may well be called a strange process of idealisation and spiritualisation. The caste economy gave to these new acquisitions the outer forms of the Aryan social structure ; the law and disciplines of the *ashramas* communicated to them the inner spirit of the Aryan culture. The moment these non-Aryan peoples received the badge of the Brahminical social economy and accepted the disciplines of the Brahminical culture, they became, both in form and substance, part and limb of the great Aryan community. The priests of the non-Aryan communities, when adopted into the Aryan fold, became Brahmins not merely in name, but also in fact ; and though preserving all the old peculiarities of their tribal or racial laws and customs, became in every respect the absolute equals of the holiest of the Aryan Brahmins. The same thing happened also in regard to the other castes. The different castes in the different regions thus fully retained all their old, and even non-Aryan peculiarities, after their assimilation by the Aryan community. The Brahmin of Madras or Bombay, therefore, differs in many respects from those of Bengal or Kashmir. Things and usages absolutely prohibited to the Brahmins of one region, are freely permitted to those of another. Oftentimes the personal and the civil laws of the people, thus brought into the Aryan fold, were allowed to remain more or less intact. But all these endless diversities notwithstanding, there was social equality between the members of the same caste in the different areas. As the Aryan society absorbed the different classes of the non-Aryan society, by putting upon them its own caste-order seal, in accordance with their respective places and functions in their old community, so also the gods of these non-Aryan peoples were accepted into the Aryan pantheon, being interpreted according to Aryan ideas and conceptions, while even their special liturgies and worships were also retained, sometimes in their original forms, and sometimes with modifications, but always with a new and spiritual interpretation, for the special use and profit of the newly acquired communities. And when a nation grows in this way, it must necessarily retain almost endless diversities of customs and rituals, faiths and worships, sacraments and disciplines, inside its broad and catholic unity. This is the real psychology of the perplexing diversitiy of our culture and civilisation.

Aryan Methods of Unification

But while granting the utmost freedom to the

different communities not merely to maintain but even to develop their respective peculiarities, both of thought and institutions, the Aryan nation-builders took great care to ordain certain rules and rituals, certain sacraments and ceremonials, that were binding upon all sections of the expanding Aryan society, and that sought to preserve and strengthen their fundamental unity. The sacrament of the *Upanayana*, popularly known as the ceremony through which every boy of the first three castes, called the twice-born castes, is vested with the Brahminical insignia of the so-called sacred thread, is binding on all the Brahmins, the Kshatriyas and the Vaisyas to whatever region they may belong, and whatever may be their faith or their personal law or local customs. The daily repetition of the Vedic text known as the *Gayatri* is another obligation of this type. A Brahmin may worship any god he likes, may belong to any sect or denomination, whether old or new, but he must repeat the *Gayatri* every day. There are local gods and sectarian sanctities, but there are a few gods who receive universal homage, and some places that are sacred to every Hindu of any denomination. And it is significant that these sacred places, visited by devout pilgrims of every sect and from every region, are found very widely spread over the whole continent. Haridwar, near the source of the Ganges, Prayag (modern Allahabad) and Banaras, in northern India ; Gaya in Bihar ; Nasik in Central India ; Dvarka in Kathiwad ; and Kumbhakonam and Rameshvar in southern India,—are some of these sacred places. Pilgrims from every Indian region are used to visiting these distant places, and thus are able to visualise the unity of their sacred country—their *karmabhumi* or the land where they have to work for the attainment of merit and the destruction of demerit. And by this means they carry the experiences of different social and religious lives of distant parts of the country to their respective homes, to at once broaden their outlook and strengthen the sense of national unity in them. But the most significant formula of national unity invented by the Indo-Aryans is found in the sacred text which every Hindu has to use, whether he be a Brahmin or a non-Brahmin, each time he bathes or sits down to worship his God—the text for the sacrificial purification of water. It runs thus :

Gangecha Jamunechaiva Godavari Sarasvatee
Narmmada Sindhu Kaveri jalesmin sannidhim kuru

And it means :—May the Ganges, the Jumna,

the Godavari, the Sarasvatee, the Narmada, the Sindhu or the Indus, and the Kaveri enter into this water. These are the great rivers of the Indian continent. They cover practically the entire riparian system of this great land. It is along the course of these great rivers, that the sacred stream of Aryan culture flowed over this land. In the days before the introduction of the railways, the great rivers were the highways of commerce and culture. This is why they are so sacred to the Indo-Aryan. And the Hindu wherever he may be in this wide country, by repeating this text during his daily baths and worships, remembers the unity of his country and his people. And all these are conclusive proofs of the fact that at a very early period of our history we had fully realised a very deep, though complex, kind of organic unity at the back of all the apparent diversities and multiplicities of our land and people.

Hindu India

India was far more than a mere geographical expression or entity, even from the earliest period of Hindu history. You will find ample evidences of it in our great epics. In fact, you find in the Mahabharata itself the clearest possible evidence of a very extensive and conscious attempt to work up a great Hindu confederacy that would unite the whole continent in one powerful and well-ordered federal whole. This was clearly the motif of the Bharata war. Sree Krishna was the divine stage-manager of this great historic drama. He is to a very large extent the *dieu ex machina* of this national plot. And Sree Krishna was, without doubt, the first and the greatest empire-builder that not only India, but the world has as yet known. But the empire that he desired to build up in India was very different from what has been known as such in other parts of the world. It was not to be an empire based upon the subjection of extensive territories and immense populations to a centralised government represented by a small class or coterie. His was the true ideal of an empire. The central aim of the Bharata war, which Sree Krishna in some sense himself brought about, was not to acquire territory, but to work out a great socio-political synthesis in India, upon the basis of *Dharma*, and thus to combine the numerous races and divergent cultures of the continent into one organic whole. And this ideal of a spiritually-inspired and culturally-combined federation that Sree Krishna had in view in directing the Bharata war, was fairly, if not fully, realised in ancient Hindu history. Buddhistic imperialism, under Chandragupta and Asoka, whose suzereinty was acknowledged from the confines of Burma on the east to the very heart of modern Afghanistan on the west, helped materially to further develop and consolidate this fundamental Indian unity, which had commenced to be worked up from even before the great Bharata War.

Mahomedan India

India was thus a great country, united in a common culture, though divided into many provinces and principalities, possessing a common life, though following diverse laws and customs, and pursuing, through diverse ways, a common spiritual and social ideal,—when the Mahomedans came to us. The Moslem rulers of India came into these invaluable inheritances of the Hindus. And they added new and equally valuable elements to the old national life and consciousness of the country. The old Hindu unity was essentially socio-religious. It was the unity of common spiritual ideals and disciplines. The Mahomedans came, however, with a different culture and a different order of experience to us. The genius of Islam is essentially Semitic. The peculiarity of the Semitic race-consciousness consists in its dominating legalism. Its emphasis is more on the positive than on the imaginative and emotional elements of life.

The exquisite emotionalism and idealism of Islam, as found in the art and literature of Persia, is the contribution of Aryan race-consciousness to this great world-religion. These elements were native to the soil of India. India had no need of Islam for the deepening of her spiritual or emotional life. What her Moslem rulers did was to add certain positive contents of the national life to her old consciousness and culture. Islamic law and administration helped, through these contributions, to simultaneously deepen and broaden the foundations of our national life and unity. To the old community of socio-religious life and ideals, the Mahomedans now added new elements of administrative and political unity. There were still many more or less independent principalities in the land, but practically all owned at least a kind of nominal allegiance to the central government at Delhi. Local and communal laws, as well as denominational customs and rituals still held sway over the people, but all irrespective of caste or community, became equally subject to certain laws and obligations, known only to Islam. The whole country became subject to one criminal law, the Mahomedan, and to one common judiciary, the Kadi and Kazi. Local imposts and provincial finances practically remained as under the Hindu administrations, but a wide and general system of imperial revenue and taxation was imposed upon all the country subject to the central government at Delhi. As in the hey-day of the Roman Empire, all roads in Europe led, they say, to Rome ; so in the hey-day of the Mogul Empire in India, all roads led to Delhi or Agra. The old unity of India and the ancient national life and consciousness of her multitudinous peoples, were thus considerably deepened and enlarged under Moslem rule.

The British came into all these glorious inheritances of their predecessors, the Hindus and the Mahomedans of India. They have not had to create any new national consciousness in the country : but have simply been adding fresh elements to the old, old life and unity of the land. India had ceased to be a mere geographical expression or entity long before the advent of the British East India Company among us. It had been a social unit long long before the Mahomedans came to her with a new cry and culture, to give her something that she lacked and to receive in return from her something that they themselves lacked. The old Indian unity, inspite of local, communal and denominational differences and diversities was still to some extent, not in its details but in its general outline and outlook, more or less homogenous. It was at any rate what may be called a Hindu unity. This unity had been worked up through the subsumption of just one or two comparatively developed, and numerous nebulous and undeveloped, that is undifferentiated, cultures under one dominating ideal and principle supplied by the Aryan consciousness and culture. The Mahomedans came, however, with a fully developed and world-conquering culture. The necessity of the situation required, therefore, a higher synthesis than what had been previously worked up. Indian unity, always more or less of a federal type, now became still more pronouncedly so. Hinduism, ever ready to accept and accommodate whoever came to her in the name of God and could furnish positive proofs of true spiritual acquisitions, made room now for many a Moslem saint and devotee in her invisible temple. New Hindu cults, like those associated with the holy names of Nanak and Kabir, came into being in the attempt to work out some sort of a synthesis between Hinduism and Islam. And as the naturally-broad spirit of Hindu culture was further broadened through Moslem contact, so the old Semitic legalism and absolutism of Islam also considerably relaxed its native rigidities through its contact with the spirit of Hindu universalism. Indian Mahomedanism assumed a form and developed certain characters and tendencies unknown to the rest of the Islamic world. Thus we had, under the Moguls, a new India, larger, broader, at once more differentiated and more united, a more organic, though not yet fully organised, national life and consciousness than what we had before. The British came to this India ; and not to an unorganised, unconscious, and undeveloped chaos, having simply a geographycal entity. And in view of all this, it is unpardonable ignorance to say that India was always and still is a mere geographical expression, and the Indians have always been and still are a chaotic congregation of many peoples, an incoherent and heterogenous collection of tribes and races, families and castes, but not in any sense a nation.

LETTER III

INDIA : THE MOTHER

Cultural Unity and National Unity

In your last letter you raise the very pertinent question, whether cultural unity is the same as national unity. "Many Europeans," you say, "would not deny that under the Hindus, India had a common culture. So has Europe to-day. But yet the Europeans are not one nation. How, then, can the old cultural unity of India prove her national unity also ?"

I am glad that you have raised this question. It drew my attention to a thing that I might have otherwise overlooked.

I fully admit that the bases of European nationalities are not really a common culture. Of course, the members of the different nations in Europe, as elsewhere, are participators in a common culture, but that culture is not specifically their own, it is not national, but continental. For, culturally all Europe is one : and even America is not different from Europe in this respect. There are differences of national characteristiscs, as between the British and the French, or between the Germans and the Russians, or the Italians and the Spaniards.

But there is really little or on difference in culturals ideals between them. There is practically one religion, one social economy, one ideal of life and art, one broad culture and civilisation all over Europe and America. Racially also there is practically little difference between one European nation and another. Yet they are not one people, but a group of many distinct peoples, who go by the common name of the European. Apparently it is the same in India also. There may be one culture in India, but yet many separate nationalities.

But let us see what really constitutes nationality. We know that Europe has developed a particular type of nationhood. In Europe a nation means a group of humans who (i) occupy a common territory; (ii) are subjects of a common state; (iii) generally speak one language; (iv) profess one religion, though there may be sectarian differences; (v) have one common social economy; and (v) participate in a common culture. These are accepted connotations of nationality in Europe. As I have already said, some of these elements are even common to all the Western nations. These are, religion, culture and social economy. Thus the really distinguishing features of European nationalities are territorial and and political unity. The differentiating factors between one nationality and another in Europe are, therefore, not cultural but geographical. Of course, some kind of territorial unity is an essential factor of nationality everywhere. As our physical organisation is the fundamental material basis of our personal lives, so territorial unity is to national lives. This fundamental basis of nationality is common to both Europe and Asia. It is a universal factor of national life. The fundamental difference between European nationalism and Indian natianalism lies in the excessive emphasis of the one on territorial and of the other on cultural unity. The emphasis on territorial unity in national differentiations when it is associated with a general community of religious ideals and social economies between different neighbouring nations, means ultimately an excessive emphasis upon couflicts of mere temporal interests. It is these temporal interests that divide the modern European nations from one another. Economic conflicts, industrial competitions, greedy rivalries for the acquisition of unappropriated territories and the possession of unexplored markets,—these are what have contributed to the quickening and preservation of nationalism in Europe, and have kept the European nations apart from one another. But for these carnal conflicts, Europe might well have been to-day as much a nation, as India was under the Hindus, and what she is essentially even to-day.

The Federal Type of Nationality

But the type of nationhood which Europe would then develop would be different from what exists in Europe at the present time. There is an element of homogeniety in all the European nations at the present time, which is absent in India. This homogeniety is due to the peculiar course of evolution which these nations have passed through. In the earliest stages of social evolution, nations grow through the accretion of more or less fluid tribal organisations ; and owing to this fluidity, the tribal fusion becomes easy, and the resulting nation absolutely homogenous in all respects. This was the general process of nation-building in ancient Europe. So also it must have been in the earliest stages of the evolution of the Aryan community in India. The original Aryan type was also completely homogenous, like all the older types of nations. When, even at a somewhat later stage of social evolution, different nebulous tribes combine to form one larger tribe or a nation, under the influence of some one particular and comparatively more developed tribe or culture, they gradually adopt the language, the religion, the social ideal and economy of this dominating community. It is thus that there grows a kind of homogeniety even in these new social units also. This is really the cause of the homogeniety of those European nations that are racially heterogenous. But at a later stage of social evolution when not fluid tribal cultures, but advanced and developed nations, first come into contact and conflict with one another, and then, in course of time, under pressure of new historic forces, combine to form one united nation, this early homogenous character can hardly be maintained.

Owing, however, to the peculiar conditions of social evolution in Europe, since the breakup of the Roman Empire, the old homogenous character of nationality was not seriously disturbed even when comparatively advanced tribes combined to form national units. Europe had been already Christianised. Christianity meant not merely a common religious creed, but also a common social ideal. It is not merely a creed but essentially a culture. And owing to this fact, the fusion of even advanced communities did not violently destroy the old homogenous character of nationhood. But still there are many heterogenous elements even in the most consolidated nationalities of Europe. The British people, for instance, are by no means homogenous. The British are a composite nation, the component entities being English,

Welsh and Scotch. England has, no doubt, tried her utmost, for many centuries past, to crush the independent national consciousness of both Wales and Scotland. But has she completely succeeded in her attempt? She imposed her own language upon these two peoples, thus practically killing the old Gaelic and Celtic languages and literatures. But all these repressions notwithstanding, the national consciousness of neither Wales nor Scotland has been entirely killed. The cry to-day in both these countries, as you know better than I do,—is for an independent national existence, inside a true Federation of the British Empire. What both Wales and Scotland, and even Ireland, desire is not simply political self-government, but rather a self-contained and self-controlled national life, which will give them free scope for the development of those mental, moral and spiritual characteristics in which these peoples stand differentiated from others, and thereby enable them to make their special contribution to the general life and culture of Universal Humanity. The Home Rule propaganda, as you know, does not mean a demand for national isolation, but rather for a healthy international federation. And it indicates the nature of the coming type of social evolution.

The Old Indian Type, Federal

India, my child, had developed this federal type of nationality ages and ages ago. In Christendom, this federal idea is of very recent growth. It was first applied to the organisation of the United States of America. But even this application was only to one part of the social life, namely, the organisation of the State. The political constitution of America is alone federal. But India had developed a much wider and fuller type of federalism. Our religion, as I have already told you, has been organised after the federal ideal. Hinduism is not one uniform religious culture, nor based upon one universal creed or one particular system of dogmas, like Christanity or Islam, or Buddhism ; but it is a group of diverse theologies and dogmas and disciplines and rituals and worships, all moved, however, by one common spirit and pursuing one common ideal. Our social economy has similarly been of a distinct federal character. The Hindu society is really a group of many communities, each practically independent of the others and autonomous within its own sectional or communal or caste life, but combined with the others in the pursuit of a common ideal, namely, the revelation of God in man. Our States were also of this federal type. Each village community was autonomous within the limits of the communal life and concerns of the village, but formed part of the larger life of the province or principality. And sometimes even these provinces and principalities combined to form large confederacies, which, while leaving all local autonomies absolutely intact, combined them into one great organic whole for the pursuit of larger ends and the realisation of more general purposes. This is really the advanced type of social organisation towards which humanity is slowly moving. In fact, India furnishes a model of that Universal Federation, the Federation of the World, which is the dream of the seers and prophets of modern Western humanity.

Characteristics of Western Patriotism

And all these peculiarities of our history and evolution have helped to develop a type of patriotism among us which is almost unknown in Europe. Owing to the fundamental unity of the religion and culture of Europe, the different nations of your great continent are separated from one another by considerations of mere material interests. And when the carnal conflicts of mean material interests divide one people from another, and supply the motif of their nationality and patriotism, the national character develops all those traits with which we are familiar in Europe. In the first place, patriotism, evoked by the conflicts of mere material interests, naturally becomes much keener and stronger than when its appeal lies to man's higher instincts and ideals. Constituted as man is, his passion for material advantages and possessions is naturally much stronger than for things moral or spiritual. And owing to the predominant secular reference of his national life and composition, the European's passion for his country has always been stronger than what we have ever known in India. On the other hand, patriotism, inspired by considerations of material gain and brought into play through conflicts of mean secular interests, must inevitably become narrow and selfish, intolerant and aggressive. This is, to a very large extent, the general character of patriotism that drives the great nations of Europe to so perpetually "snarl at each other's heels." And it is for this very reason also that in Europe, love of the Fatherland has not yet visibly broadened into any real love of humanity. This type of narrow, selfish and pathological patriotism was never developed in ancient India.

The Hindu Ideal of Patriotism

Our highest ideal of love and devotion to our

country is to be found in our conception of our land as Mother. On the face of it, the conception is not peculiar to India. Other peoples have also addressed their land in the terms of the parental relation. The ancient Romans called their country, *patria* or the fatherland. Germany is in our day addressed as the Fatherland by the Germans. We too have the expression motherland among us. *Jananee Janmabhumischa Sargadapee Gareeyasee.* "The mother and the motherland are greater than heaven itself," says a Sanskrit text. I cannot tell you just now whether the expression *janmabhumi* or motherland is a modern or an ancient usage in Sanskrit. The text I have quoted is, however, undoubtedly very modern. But even if we had the term motherland in our ancient language and literature, it was not the highest expression of our ideal of what is known as patriotism in Europe.

Expressions like fatherland are clearly metaphorical. There is an element of poetical imagination behind them. The imagination that clothed our conception of our country was, however, of a much superior order. It was not poetical but essentially religious. We addressed our land not merely as *janani janma-bhumi* or mother-country, but simply as Mother. I do not know of any other people who ever did so.

The real concept Mother as applied to India by her children has no metaphor behind it. Of course, most of our modern-educated people use and understand the word in a poetical and metaphorical sense. But this is because their education and environment have more or less completely divorced their thought and imagination from the ancient realities of their language and literature. There are, indeed, numerous words in common use among us to-day, that have entirely lost their original sense, owing to the loss of the genuine thought-life of the people in the wilderness of un-understood and unassimilated foreign words and concepts accumulated by our present system of education. When, for instance, we talk of *Dharma* we do not understand it to mean either law of being or sacrifices and rituals or duty, the three different senses in which the word was always used among us, but the imported concept religion. Similarly, we use the word *Niti*, which really means strategy and statecraft, for European morals. With the Europeanisation of our mind and modes of thinking even our words have been imperceptibly Europeanised. It is not at all surprising, therefore, that the original significance of the word Mother as applied to our country, has also been largely lost to many of our educated countrymen, who see nothing more sacred or serious in it than a very tender and beautiful metaphor.

It was, however, very different with those who first applied this word to their land. The Mother, in what people call the motherland, was to them not a mere idea or fancy, but a distinct personality. The woman who bore them and nursed them, and brought them up with her own life and substance was no more real a personality in their thought and idea than the land which bore and reared, and gave food and shelter to all their race. But to seize the full truth and reality of this concept you will have to study it in the light of the entire Nature Philosophy of the Hindus.

The Nature Gods of the Hindus

Nature to the Hindu was never absolutely inanimate or impersonal. But when I say this do not rush to the easy and convenient conclusion that it is only an example of what the Europeans call animism, and is therefore something which is common to primitive culture. Indeed, personally, I strongly object to the application of this term animism to even the lowest forms of human faiths or religions. The very conception is crude and absolutely empirical. Animism means really the ascription of life to non-life. Faiths that project or posit distinct personalities behind natural or material objects and phenomena are classed as animistic by Europeen thinkers. But has Europe discovered all the secrets of Nature? Can she draw the line between life and non-life? Has she been able, my child, to remove the mask of that which her children, with all the inordinate conceits of innocent childhood, so glibly talk of as "personality?" Has our much-vaunted scientific culture been able to even suggest a solution of the unfathomable mysteries of this personality? On the contrary, are not all your highest theistic thinkers and Christian divines practically doing the same thing which they treat with such superior contempt in those whom they call savage and superstitious? Do they not themselves posit a Mind, an Intelligence, a Spirit, a God, behind all the inanimities of what they write down as Nature, with a capital N? And is there any fundamental difference in kind between the animistic explanation of natural phenomena, familiar to what is called primitive culture, and the theistic explanation offered by the modern thinker and theologian? Both belong to the same class. Both posit life and intelligence and emotion and will, which really means a personality, at the back of natural phenomena that are apparently lifeless, unconscious and incapable of emotion or volition. The difference between them lies in this only, namely, that while the so-called primitive man posits numerous agencies behind phenomena, the modern Christian thinker posits not many, but One Agent behind these. And it is exceedingly doubtful whether the modern Christian explanation is more satisfactory than the old heathen explanations.

The Hindu has, from of old, posited individual entities behind different prominent and active natural objects. The sun, the moon, the earth, the sky, the winds, the phenomena of the morning and the evening twilight, the great mountains of his land, as well as all the great rivers along the course of which the stream of his national life and culture flowed from one part of the country to another,—all these had, in his thought, distinct personal entities behind them. Whether it be real or merely imaginary, the popular belief in these personalities behind natural objects and phenomena, was by no means animistic. The natural objects were never looked upon as gods. As there is a distinct difference between our own bodies and what we call our soul, which is the essence and substance of our personalities ; so there is a distinct difference between the sun-god or the moon-god, or the earth-god, etc , and the natural objects with which these are visibly associated. Having from almost prehistoric times reached the supreme spiritual consciousness of the separation of the soul from the body in the human kingdom, the Hindu found absolutely no difficulty in accepting the presence of these different divinities in different natural objects,—divinities that are as much invisible and spiritual as the soul of man. The outer objects are not really the gods, but only their bodies, just as our own bodies are not ourselves, but only our outer habiliments. And as the existence of innumerable human personalities does not destroy the Unity of the Supreme, so even the extension of the idea of similar personalities to what is called the natural order of creation, in no way destroys the Divine Unity. In fact, the Hindu's belief in gods and goddesses no more makes his religion polytheistic than the Catholic Christian's belief in angels makes Catholicism polytheistic, or the Protestant faith in the Father, the Son and the Holy Ghost makes Trinitarian Christianity tri-theistic.

Hindu Theory of Ultimate Reality

The origin of the concept Mother as applied by the Hindu to his geographical habitat must be traced, I think, to the ancient Vedic conception of the Earth-God. Subsequent speculations, instead of dissipating, on the contrary, helped very materially to deepen and vivify, this old idealism. The highest philosophical speculations of the Hindus have posited two ultimate principles, or, more correctly speaking, two final personalities in the universe ; one is called *Purusha*, the other *Prakriti*. In some shape or other, in one name or another, these dual principle are found in every Hindu system, except perhaps in that of the avowedly materialistic and atheistic schools of the Lokayatas, who had very close affinity with the Epicurians of Greece. The names *Purusha* and *Prakriti* belong specifically to the Sankhya system. At the final analysis, two ultimate principles are found in creation, one is the principle of permanence, the other of change. No rational interpretation of cosmic evolution is possible except upon the hypothesis of these two fundamental principles. All evolution means change in something which retains its identity through all changes. Like shine and shade, permanence and change always go together ; the one is unthinkable and impossible without the other. In our Sankhya system of philosophy, *Purusha* represents the principle of permanence, and *Prakriti* that of change. In the Vedantic philosophy, *Purusha* is called Isvara and *Prakriti* Maya ; the former representing the noumenal and the latter the phenomenal aspect of Reality. In the system of the Vaishnavas, Shree Krishna is *Purusha* and *Prakriti* is Radha. In the thought of the Shaivaites, *Purusha* is Shiva and *Prakriti* is Shakti. The conception of Mother associated with our geographical habitat is filiated to this old, old, universal Hindu conception of *Prakriti*; but of *Prakriti* conceived especially as Shakti.

Christian Trinity and Hindu Purusha-Prakriti

The same necessity of thought that developed the dogma or mystery of the Holy Trinity, gave rise among us to this dogma or mystery of the *Purusha* and *Prakriti*. If the Ultimate Reality be, as is admitted in every theistic system, intelligent and self-conscious, then it must have all the necessary elements of consciousness. Reason or consciousness can work only through duality. Rational or thought life is inconceivable and impossible without something to know or think of. This something must not be absolutely different from us, nor must it be absolutely identical with us. For we can never know that which we are not; all knowledge is, therefore, really self-knowledge. Nor can we know anything which is not differentiated from us. The object of our knowledge must be the same as ourselves, yet at the same time different from us. And in every act of knowledge or thought we first create, so as to say, a separation between ourselves and our object, and immediately this is done, we cancel it again. To quote a well-known saying of one of your own European philosophers, in every act of knowledge or reason, "the self separates itself from itself to return to itself to be itself." And if this be the logic of rational life, and if the Ultimate Reality, by whatever name called, whether God, or Allah, or Brahman, or Isvara, be intelligent and self-conscious, then you must posit in the very Being of that Reality an element of differentiation which, without cancelling the Divine Unity, supplies the object of Divine thought, through which the Divine realises His own consciousness. The Ultimate Reality being infinite, the object through which that Reality can realise its infinite reason, must also be infinite. As it is true of the rational, so also is it true of the emotional and the volitional life. Love also demands with a view to realise itself an object not different from, yet not absolutely identified with, the lover. This is true also of our will or volition. In all the three elements of the rational or spiritual life, the same process of the seperation of the self from itself and its return to itself, with a view to realise itself, is perpetually present. In all these there is a necessary element of differentiation. In all these our object is both different from, yet identical with, us. And if you can grasp this fact, my child, you will find absolutely no difficulty in understanding tither the truth of the Christian Trinity or our own Mystery of the *Purusha* and *Prakriti*.

Christ and Prakriti

That through which the Divine realises Himself in His Own being is called Christ by the Christians, and *Prakriti* by the Hindus. This, however, is not the historical Christ, but the Christ of the Trinity, in and through whom the Father eternally realises His Reason, His Love and His Will or Volition. The process by which the Father eternally separates Himself and retuns to Himself to be Himself, is called, in Christian theology, the Eternal Generation of Christ. It is also described as the Eternal Colloquy between the Father and the Son. All these things are more or less familiar to you. And if you study our own philosophy of the *Purusha* and *Prakriti* in the light of these Christian experiences, you will at once seize its profound truth and significance, and per chance also be confirmed in the conviction of the fundamental truth of both the highest Hindu and Christian consciousness. Our *Purusha* stands for the Father of the Christian Trinity. Our *Prakriti* stands for the Son of Christian experience. As the Father and the Son are both one yet not one, so are also our *Purusha* and *Prakriti*. As the Father realises His Reason, His Love and His Will through the Son, so does *Purusha* in our thought through *Prakriti*. As the Son is the prototype of the world, and especially of Humanity, as by Him have all things been made, so our *Prakriti* is the Regulative Idea of the universe and all things are made by Her. *Prakriti* is both the efficient and the material cause of the cosmos. What is called the Eternal Generation of Christ, in Christian experience, is called *Nitya Leela* or the Eternal Sport of the Lord in our literature. The truth is the same, though expressed differently, through different sets of symbols. The special symbol of the Christian consciousness is filial, that of the Hindu consciousness is nuptial. The Sankhya doctrine of *Prakriti*, the Vedantie doctrine of *Maya*, the Vaishnavic conception of *Shakti*,—all these represent the self-same attempt of the human mind and spirit to reach and realise the Mystery of Divine Being, which the Hebrew doctrine of Sophia, the Greek doctrine of the Logos and the Christian doctrine of the Son or Christ, sought to unveil. The ultimate rational explanation of experience has been sought by all these ancient peoples, Hindu, Hebrew, Greek and the Christians at a later period, in this supreme Divine Mystery.

Prakriti as Maya, Radha and Shakti

But though there is a fundamental unity between the general conception and philosophy of *Prakriti*, there are certain marked differences between Maya, Radha, and Shakti. *Prakriti* when sought to be seized through the logic of what may be called pure reason, is seen in its aspect of Maya. This Maya is not Illusion, as is popularly interpreted by many European scholars. Even Samkara, the father of the school of Absolute Monism in India, who is popularly cited as an authority in regard to this illusory interpretation of the phenomenal world, ignorantly ascribed to the Vedantic School of Hindu thought,—posited Maya as an element in the Being of Brahman or the Absolute. When questioned by an opponent as to "what was, before creation, the object of the knowledge of Brahman ?", Samkara replied :—"It is name and form, the indescribable entity (called Maya), which is neither different from, nor identical with, Brahman ; this we shall say." And from this it is clear that Maya is *Prakriti* as conceived in relation to the Reason of God. Radha is the same *Prakriti* conceived, however, not as a necessity of Reason, but of Love and the Emotions. The Vaishnavas describe Radha as the body of the Emotions of the Supreme, through which the *Purusha* realises his Love. Radha is *Premamayee*, or made of Love. She is both the Soul and Satisfaction of Supreme Love. Shakti, on the other hand, is not the soul of Love, but that of the Divine Will. The Hindu never calls her *Premamayee*, but only *Ichhamayee*, not the symbol and instrument of Divine Love but of Divine Will. Maya is thus the explanation of our rational experience ; Radha of our emotional experience ; Shakti of our volitional experience. And the specific function of the will is to work out what the reason or the emotions demand or desire. Reason reveals the truth of things. The emotions enjoy them. The will works to develop and perfect them. The will of the Supreme lies, therefore, at the back of both cosmic and human evolution. Shakti, as the soul of the Divine Will, is Energy in cosmic life and evolution. It is what may perhaps be called the conscience in the inner life of individual humans, the dynamic element in our ethical consciousness. It is Providence in history. In a word, it is that which works out different changes through which the universe is evolving itself. It is Raciality in the history and evolution of races.

It is the spirit of Nationality in national life and evolution.

The Problem of Personality

The Christ of the Christian Trinity is not a mere Idea, but a Person. It is through the personality of Christ that the Father realises His Own Personality. Dismiss the personality of the Son, and the personality of the Father also vanishes. Or if it is still retained, it is reduced to the objectivity of the Hebrew Godhead. The Personal God of the New Testament is impossible without the personality of Christ. Like Christ in Christian consciousness, both Radha and Shakti in Hindu conciousness are not mere ideas, but persons. It is through the personality of Radha that Krishna realises His Own Personality. It is through the personality of the same *Prakriti*, but viewed not through the emotions, but through the will, and called Shakti, that the personality of Isvara or Shiva is realised. Krishna and Shiva are really one ; the two names representing not two entities, but only two aspects of the one and the same Truth or Being. So are Radha and Shakti really One ; the two names symbolising not two Beings but one Truth and Reality, viewed from two different stand-points. Brahman represents the Ultimate Reality, in its undifferentiated and therefore impersonal aspect. Krishna represents the same Ultimate Reality, but eternally self-differentiated and, therefore, the fuller truth. Krishna is the Perfected Personality of the Absolute. In Krishna, therefore, as the Hindu Vaishnavas contend, we have a truer and fuller view of the Reality than what we get in the Brahman of the Upanishads. And Krishna of the Vaishnavas is really the same as the Shiva of the Shaivaites, only viewed in another aspect. This is the Shiva of the *Shiva-jnanabodhinee* School. And Shakti, as conceived by them, is no more an idea or abstraction than is Radha of the Vaishnava or Christ of the Christian.

Prakriti and Logos

The Hindu's conception of *Prakriti* is thus as much indicative of personality as is the Christian's conception of the *Logos.* Both Radha and Shakti, the one representing the emotional and the other the volitional aspect of the eternal self-differentiation of the Absolute, are personalities in the Being of the Deity, just as Christ is in the Christian dogma. But Radha, representing the emotional aspect of *Prakriti*, has one form only, though quite an infinity of moods. Shakti, however, has many forms. This multiformness is the essential character of the will. The will assumes a different form in working out different purposes. And one of these many forms of Shakti is what we call the Spirit of Nationality.

The Being Behind Nationality

Nationality, as you may remember, has been defined by Mazzini as the "individuality of peoples." The concept individuality involves being or personality. Mazzini spoke of Humanity as a Being. And judging from this it seems to me that Mazzini conceived Nationality also as a Being. A Being is a self-conscious intelligence that seeks to realise itself through due regulation of means to end. And if there be any intelligence behind national histories and evolutions, if historical movements be not a mere play of blind chance, if, that is, there is any law and purpose behind human history, then it is only natural to conceive a Personality behind national evolutions. In any case, the Hindu did conceive such a Personality behind his own history and evolution, and it is this Personality which he addressed as Mother in his Motherland.

And he found little or no difficulty in conceiving such a personality behind his historic evolution, because he had a much clearer grasp of the concept personality than many other peoples. Literally, as you know, *persona* means a mask ; and personality really means something that is masked, Difference of personalities does not, therefore, necessarily imply separate entities but only different appearances. The Christian also holds this belief in regard to the dogma of the Trinity. The three *persons* of the Holy Trinity are only different in hypostatis or appearance but one in ousia or essence. Owing to the predominantly monistic emphasis of Hindu thought, the Hindu can more easily understand the truth of the Christian position that different personalities do not break up the fundamental unity of Being than even many orthodox and bigoted Christians. The personality of the Mother in his motherland, therefore, does not in any way destroy, in his thought, the fundamental Unity of *Prakriti*, any more than the Personality of *Prakriti* herself destroys the Divine Unity. *Prakriti* has many forms : and in every form she is a person.

The Primal Form of the Mother

The first and primal form of the Mother is, therefore, in the very bosom of the Supreme. That is her eternal place and being. In Hindu symbolism, she is seated, in this form, on the lap of Narayana or Mahavishnu. Mahavishnu represents the first step, so to say, in the process of the eternal self-differentiation of the Absolute,—within his own being. Here the Mother is undifferentiated *Prakriti*. She is both Radha and Shakti. Here is it not our Mother as differentiated from your Mother, but the Mother of all that is to be. Here the Mother is the Mother of the unborn universe, the Spirit of Cosmic Evolution, both human and non-human.

Shakti as Jagaddhatri

It is from here, the bosom of her Lord, that Shakti starts upon her manifold functions of cosmic and social evolution. She is the Force that stands behind the evolution of the universe, working out the infinite changes through which the Absolute is progressively realising Himself in the cosmic process. As the Spirit of Race, she stands behind, and directs and controls all racial and social evolution. Her first manifestation here is in the earliest jungle-clearing stage, when man, but scarcely removed as yet from the surrounding animal creation, is engaged in a life-and-death struggle with both his physical and animal environment, to secure a slice of mother earth for his humble habitation. The Race-Spirit, or Shakti, manifests herself at this stage as a tremendous and relentless animal force, fighting and subjugating the malicious brute forces about her. The Hindu has symbolised her, at this stage, by the figure of the Goddess Jagaddhatree. Jagaddhatree rides a lion. And the lion here is symbolic of the highest animal strength and intelligence. The lion represents not merely a very superior kind of brute force, but its special characteristic is the superior combination of animal strength and intelligence. The lion here does not simply stand under Jagaddhatree, but has its fore paw upon a vanquished elephant. The elephant has preserved to us the type of the extinct mammoth. It is a reminder of the mammoth age of terrestrial history and evolution. The mammoth age was characterised by the almost complete domination of the animal over man. Man was then only a weaker animal. Evolution of man, at this stage, worked itself out almost completely through the conflict of the brute in man with the brute in his fearful animal surroundings.

In Shakti, as symbolised by Jagaddhatree, there is apparently no reference to tribal conflicts. The setting of Jagaddhtree is not in human habitations, but rather in wild mountain scenery, where Nature reigns in all her terrific luxuriance, amidst yet more terrific animal life and activities. Signs of murderous struggle are there, but it is the struggle with animals and not yet with men.

Shakti as Kali

The next stage of racial or social evolution is marked by fierce tribal conflicts. Man has, by this time, partially conquered a portion of the earth from the animals, and has made it fit for his habitation, The struggle with wild Nature and wilder animals is to a very large extent over. Now the main emphasis is not on his competitions with wild animals, or with the fatal luxuriance of the vegetable kingdom, but rather with brother man. This is the stage of tribal conflicts. And Shakti or the Spirit of Raciality or Nationality as revealed at this stage is symbolised by the Hindu Goddess Kalee. Here we have the clearest symbolisation of a pure human conflict ; but the conflict is on the purely animal plane. Kalee rides on no animal. She is without any adornments except the dipping heads of men whom she has herself killed. Her setting is in the heart of the bloody desolations of war. She is dark with anger, and unconscious of the terrible carnage in which she is engaged. Yet, even at this stage of universal war and carnage, the Hindu could not absolutely lose his innate sense of the spiritual and the universal, or his consciousness of the fact that, even all this cruelty and carnage notwithstanding, there is goodness and love in creation The aim and objective of evolution, whatever may be its passing and apparent phases, is not to kill but to save, not to destroy but to develop, this principle of love and goodness in the world. So Kalee, this fearful Goddess, revelling in carnage, adorned with the skulls of the killed, covered with blood, darkened by all the passions of a competing, quarrelling, fighting, killing humanity, —is still standing on Shiva or the Good. But Shiva lies prostrate at her feet !

A popular Hindu story says that when Kalee was engaged in this work of destruction, she so completely forgot herself that she did not stop with the killing and conquest of her enemies, but threatened, in her passion for war and carnage, to work universal ruin. And it was then that Shiva, the symbol of the good, who alone in all the worlds could stand the passion of the dread Goddess, threw himself down at her feet, and thus brought her back to herself. Kalee, therefore, stands naked and fearful, drunk with the lust of war and blood, on the prostrate form of Shiva, her Lord and Lover.

Shakti As Durga

But this is not the final stage of racial or national evolution. The conflicts between the barbaric tribalities, yet but scarcely removed from the animal kingdom, is succeeded by the more organised but therefore nonetheless severe conflicts, between more advanced nations. Here the conflict is between competing colours and rival cultures. Here the Mother is revealed not merely in the animal life and activities of humanity, but in the far more developed and organised national or social organisms. This is the stage when the Hindu symbolised the Mother or Shakti in the form of Durga, popularly called the ten-handed Goddess. The spirit of Nationality is here fully developed. The social life is completely organised, social functions are clearly differentiated. The rational autonomy of the different departments of life,—military, economic, æsthetic, spiritual, has been fairly established. Yet all these are united in and subordinated to the unity of the national and the social life. Durga represents this perfected type of nationhood. She is the Soul of National Life and Unity. With her ten hands, she joins all the ten points of the compass in her, symbolising the territorial unity of the nation's body. Nay more, her ten hands symbolise also the unity of the whole globe. They are symbols of general terrestrial interrelations and unity. She too, like Jagaddhatree, rides a lion. It shows that the spirit of the nation is related vitally and organically to the animal kingdom about her. But they are no longer, as in the early jungle-clearing stage, her enemies and competitors for the possession of mother-earth, but her help and instruments. Brute force is not eliminated, but has been absolutely brought under control. The lion is here the willing slave of the Mother, rendering not sullen but joyous service unto Her, not fearing but loving Her with all the love of his royal nature. But unlike both Jagaddhatree and Kalee, Durga does not stand simply by herself. That was the Mother's form in the earlier undifferentiated stages of social and national evolution. Jagaddhatree and Kalee represent those earlier stages. As symbolising a much more advanced and developed, that is, at once more differentiated and more united, national life,—Durga is supported on one side by Lakshmee, the goddess of wealth, the symbol and spirit of the economic and industrial life and activities of the nation, on the other side, by Sarasvatee, the goddess of learning and the arts, the symbol and spirit of intellectual and æsthetic life and activities. But the economic, the æsthetic and the intellectual activities of any people do not sum up and exhaust the whole range of their social functions and life. The economic activities bring them into almost perpetual conflicts with their neighbouring nations. These conflicts arose in the earliest stages of social evolution from the competitions and rivalries of neighbouring tribes for territorial expansion and possession. In subsequent stages these arise through industrial competitions between one nation and another. And these conflicts require, for the protection of the economic life and freedom of the people, another department of national activities, namely, the military. It is the national army that up till now has everywhere protected the basal economic life and organisation of every nation. Lakshmee or the goddess of wealth or earthly possessions, both in territory and merchandise, has therefore always to be duly protected by Kartikeya or the god of war. If Lakshmee represents the economic life of the nation, Kartikeya represents its military life. Both are equally necessary to a healthy and self-contained national existence. On the other hand, the æsthetic and intellectual life of every nation also requires for its preservation and healthy evolution the spirit of true wisdom as its guide and *guru*. Science and art, without the spirit of wisdom or universal culture, become abortive and barren. They fail absolutely of their high and lofty purposes, unless guided and controlled by wisdom. Where "knowledge comes but wisdom lingers," there the inevitable result is loss of intellectual vigour and spiritual vision. There science becomes charlatanism, and the arts sensual and vicious. In the perfected life of the nation, the ideal that is sought to be symbolised by our Goddess Durga,— the economic life must be protected by the legitimate strength of the arm, and the intellectual and æsthetic life must be guided and controlled, uplifted and spiritualised, by the spirit of the highest wisdom. Ganapati, the so-called Elephant-God, who stands next to Sarasvatee in the group of figures representing Durga, represents this spirit of wisdom. This is why Durga, with all these, who are one with her, her own progeny and family, has always symbolised the fully realised national life and consciousness in the religious imagination and symbolism of the Hindus. Durga is a form of *Prakriti*, like Jagaddhatree or Kalee. While these two represent, however, the spirit of national life and evolution at the first two stages, Durga represents the same spirit at the last and fully evolved stage of that life.

The Nationalist Interpretation of Durga

These are the many symbols through which we have been worshipping the Mother for countless centuries. It is a strange symbolism, at once both cosmic and social, both national and humanitarian. The Mother whom we worship as Jagaddhatree, or Kalee, or Durga,—and she has many other names also, the great Mahratta nation-builder Shivaji worshipped her as Bhavanee,—is, however, no mere racial symbol or deity. There is a mysterious combination of the particular and the universal in this, as in almost every other, symbolism of the Hindu religion. It is, therefore, that it appeals to all classes of our people, and is suited to the temperament, culture and character, both intellectual and spiritual, of almost all men. The modern multitudes in India do not, perhaps, fully realise the profound nationalist reference of these cults. They look upon Jagaddhatree, Kalee, Durga, and all the other gods and goddesses of popular worship, as forms of the Deity, the Author and Governor of the universe. To them Jagaddhatree, Kalee, Durga, Bhavanee, and the other gods and goddesses associated with the cult of Shiva and Shakti, as well as those associated with the cult of Vishnu and Radha, are all simply manifestations of the Lord and Protector of the universe. But the multitudes everywhere do the same. It is only the few in all countries and in every religion, who are able to rise to a full consciousness of the inner meaning and significance of the current dogmas and symbols of their religion. And the deeper meaning of no religion should be sought for in the mechanical practices and the traditional and unconscious faiths of its votaries. It is the same with Hinduism as it is with Christianity or Islam or any other religion.

How many among those who not only profess but even teach and preach Christianity, have any understanding or appreciation of the meaning of the Christian dogmas of the Incarnation and the Trinity? The masses attend the church, accept the sacraments, repeat the prayers, and try, so far as may be, to follow the Ten Commandments, even if they do so much,—and think that their religious duty is fairly discharged. It is the same with my people also. The multitudes observe the outer forms of their religion, but do not understand, and harldy ever care either to enter into the deeper meaning of what they say or do. It is in the saints and sages, it is in the general course of the historical development of the dogmas and symbols of every religion, in the progressive exegesis and interpretations of these in the light of expanding and deepening spiritual experience, that the true meaning and significance of these dogmas and symbols must be looked for and seized. It is the Christian Fathers to whom one must go for a true interpretation of the Christian mysteries, and not to the catechist or the colporteur. It is in the history of the Christian doctrine that you must seek for its rational meaning and purpose. So also in regard to our own mysteries and dogmas and doctrines. The true meaning of the cult of the Mother, as I have been trying to explain to you, must be sought for in the course of the historic evolution of it, as well as in the meaning discovered by saints and devotees in their inner spiritual experiences, and not in the extraneous and blind criticisms of the outsider who can, at his best, apply only either the cannons of formal logic and the lower intellect, or the generalisations of his own particular spiritual experience, for unlocking its mystery.

The History of the Durga Cult

And if we look into the history or tradition of the Durga cult we at once see its profound racial or national reference. According to the Hindu legends, Suratha was the first to inaugurate the worship of Durga. Ask the most illiterate Hindu in the most backward village of Bengal, as to how Durga came to be worshipped, and he will mention the name of Suratha as the first worshipper of Durga. Suratha belonged to the early *Satya-Yuga* or golden age. His was the regular worship. But the current worship of Durga was started by Rama, the hero of the Ramayana. And Durga was worshipped by him ages after Suratha, not at the time appointed by the latter, but at a different time, and so rather irregularly, during a serious crisis in the progress of his war with Ravana, which forms the theme of the Ramayana. The story of the Ramayana clearly refers to a very vital conflict between the Aryan culture of the North and the non-Aryan culture of the South of India. And it was during this vital conflict that the Mother was awakened untimely, to help and save her people. And all these are, it seems to me, ample justification for the nationalist interpretation of the Durga cult. This interpretation is further confirmed by the whole story of the portion known as Chandee in the Markandeya Purana. This story describes a great conflict between the Devas and the Asuras. The Devas were the representatives and protectors of Aryan culture. The Asuras evidently represented a different and opposing culture and community. It was during this struggle that the Devas created Chandee, one of the manifestations of Durga, out of their combined strength and merit, each of the Devas giving a portion of his own soul and strength for the purpose. She was, thus, the product of the collective life and strength of the godly community. In other words, Chandee was the manifestation of the Spirit of the hierarchy of the gods. And when we consider all these, the conclusions presented here regarding the inner meaning and significance of the Durga cult and the whole range of symbolism associated with it, seems irresistible.

But though there seems to be little doubt that the original meaning of the Durga cult was essentially racial or national, it soon became, as everything did in the consciousness of the Hindu, universalised The Mother of the Race or Nation soon became the Mother of Humanity. The presiding deity of the race and nation became identified with the Lord and Author of the universe. So Jagaddhatree, Kalee, Durga, and all other names and symbols of Shakti, came to be addressed as Jaganmata or the World-Mother. They became the Mother of all. And this universalisation helped considerably to weaken the old and original significance of the Shakti cult as what may be called the cult of Nationality or Patriotism in India.

The New Patriotism

But while to some extent it was weakened in intensity, it gained very considerably in breadth and liberality, by the universalisation. It helped to prevent the unfortunate divorce between the life of the nation and the larger life of humanity in and through which alone can all national lives and cultures find their highest and most perfect fulfilment and realisation,—the kind of divorce that has happened in Europe.

The reawakening of national consciousness and aspirations in India in our own time has revived the ancient idealism of the Shakti cult, and Durga, Kalee, Jagaddhatree, Bhavanee and all the other great forms and symbols used by the Hindu Shakti-worshippers, have received a new meaning. All these old and traditional gods and goddesses who had lost their hold upon the modern mind, have been re-installed with a new historic and nationalist interpretation in the mind and soul of the people. Hundreds of thousands of our people have commenced to hail their motherland to-day as Durga, Kalee, Jagaddhatree. These are no longer mere mythological conceptions or legendary persons or even poetic symbols. They are different manifestations of the Mother. This Mother is the Spirit of India. This geographical habitat of ours is only the outer body of the Mother. The earth that we tread on is not a mere bit of geological structure. It is the physical embodiment of the Mother. Behind this physical and geographical body there is a Being, a Personality, —the Personality of the Mother. These mountains, these rivers, these extensive plains and lofty plateus, are all witnesses unto the life and love of our race, in and through which the very life and love of the Mother have sought and found uninterrupted and progressive expression. Our history is the sacred biography of the Mother. Our philosophies are the revelations of the Mother's mind. Our arts—our poetry and our painting, our music and our drama, our architecture and our sculpture, all these are the outflow of the Mother's diverse emotional moods and experiences. Our religion is the organised expression of the soul of the Mother. The outsider knows her as India. The outsider sees only her outer and lifeless physical frame. The outsider sees her as a mere bit of earth, and looks upon her as only a geographical expression and entity. But we, her children, know her even to-day as our father and their fathers had done before, for countless generations, as a Being, as a manifestation of *Prakriti*, as our mother and the Mother of our race. And we have always worshipped and do still worship her as such.

It is, I know, exceedingly difficult, if it be not abosolutely impossible, for the European or American to clearly understand or fully appreciate this strange idealisation of our land, which has given birth to this cult of the Mother among us. Some view it as rank superstition, and some view it as sinister fanaticism. No one has as yet seized, I am afraid, its supreme spiritual significance. And you need not be at all surprised at this. For this cult of the Mother is based upon the peculiarly Hindu conception of what is called the Motherhood of God. Christianity has preached the Fatherhood of God. The highest Christian piety finds expression in realising God as Father. In all the extensive literature of Christianity there is no attempt to realise God as Mother. The Hindu has always done so. The Hindu cult of the Mother is no doubt very largely associated with the conception of *Prakrti*. But in his inner spiritual consciousness the Hindu has realised the Motherhood of God not as a philosophic speculation but as a reality. All our concepts of the Universal are primarily derived from the particularities of personal experience. The Fatherhood of God is, thus, derived from our experiences of human fatherhood,—first in our own fathers, and second, directly, in our own fatherhood when God blesses us with children. Those who have not really known and loved their own fathers themselves, cannot truly know and realise what the Fatherhood of God is. Similarly, it is in the concrete experiences of motherhood in our own mothers, first dimly as through a glass, and next in the motherhood of our own wives in which we ourselves also so largely participate,—directly and almost face to face,—that we can see and seize the motherhood of God. Besides these two human, personal and primary manifestations of the divine motherhood, there are other manifestations also, in Nature, and in Society. Is not the land we live in as much a symbol of the divine motherhood even as our own mothers or the mothers of our children are ? We are born unto this land. It receives us into its bosom even as our human mothers do. It supports our life with its own substance even as the nursing mother supports the growing life of her own baby. This land is literally the mother of our physical existence. It is indeed the physical body of the soul of our land and nation. Even so is the Society to which we belong, of which this land is the geographical habitat, the vehicle and instrument of the intellectual and spiritual life of the mother-god. From this society we receive all our mental and spiritual nourishment almost from day to day. And thus, in every way, we are nourished by, dependent upon, draw the strength and inspiration of our physical and mental life from this complex being, at once physical and spiritual, geographical and social, which we call and tenderly worship as Mother in our motherland. This being is as much a revelation of the motherhood of God as are our human mothers. This is the spiritual basis of the cult of the Mother among us. It is therefore that our love of our land and people is an organic part of our ideal of the love of God. It is not, like the secular patriotism of Europe, at all a mere civic sentiment.

The cult of the Mother among us is by no means a political cult. The political propaganda with which the cry of *Bande Mataram* or Hail Mother, has recently been associated, is not in any sense an organic element of the real cult of the Mother or Motherland. It is a purely accidental association. And this cult of the Mother is in no way connected with the impious excesses for which this political propaganda, though in a very limited and sectional aspect, may be held partly responsible. The type of the patriotism that stands really at the back of these excesses is not Hindu or Indian, but essentially an imitation of foreign ideas and ideals, the fruit of the uncritical and undiscriminating study of foreign histories. The real cult of the Mother among us is part of our general spiritual culture. It is the idealisation and spiritualisation of the collective life and functions of our society. It is the apotheosis of our race-spirit and national organism. It is organically related to our highest conceptions of Humanity.

This Humanity is represented in our thought as Narayana or Mahavishnu. Narayana is an emanation of the Supreme. He is a Being, only differentiated from the Absolute. He is an element of the very Being of God. Both individual humans, as well as the collective entity called Humanity, are equally manifestations of Narayana. They are both equally divine. The one is inseparable from the other, and both from God. And the original form of the Mother, as I have told you, is on the lap of Mahavishnu,—the Nation resting eternally in Humanity. The true cult of the Mother is, therefore, with us as much a cult of Nationality as of Humanity. And it is because of this essential universalism that this cult of the Mother is so vital a part of our highest religious symbolism and spiritual culture.

LETTER IV

RELIGIOUS INDIA

It is only natural that you should be surprised to find such strange affinities between Hinduism and Christianity, as was indicated in my last letter. But, my child, in judging thoughts and systems that are apparently different from that with which we may have been associated, we usually forget that despite these outer differences and conflicts, the mind that works through these is one. All our thoughts and speculations are the efforts of that one mind, under different circumstances and in different environments ; and, consequently, provided the problems are the same, the solution that the mind may arrive at in regard to these problems must also be, though not in form but in any case in essence, the same. Besides the Christian dogma of the Trinity is admittedly the discovery of the Greek mind, which, as I pointed out to you while discussing the Indian and the European temperament, as you may remember, is structurally the same as the Hindu mind. But even where there are structural differences between the thought of one people and another, even there you will find a high level of spiritual life and thought in both the communities, where their sages and their seers speak the same truths though in diverse languages and through different sets of symbolism. It is only the camp-followers of different prophets and teachers, who, failing to understand and visualise the profound meaning of the teachings of their masters, and therefore mistaking the words for the thoughts and the outer forms for the inner spirit, or, in their pride of intellect, identifying personal opinions with universal truth and inference with fact, create all the sectarian and denominational conflicts that mark the history of human religion almost everywhere.

Buddhism and Hinduism

Nowhere, I think, have these conflicts been so few and so little ferocious as in India. And perhaps the one root reason of this rare phenomenon is to be found in the fact that the dominant religion of India, Hinduism, is not a credal religion like Christianity or Islam. Buddhism that arose out of the early Vedic religion, as a movement of protest against the excessive and soul-killing ritualism of the time, is no doubt a credal religion. But yet it differs very fundamentally from the two other credal systems that the world has known. There are two things which distinguish Buddhism from both Christianity and Islam. The first is its strong psychological emphasis, and the second is the absence of that absolutism which is characteristic of both Christianity and Islam. If there be any religion which may claim to be predominantly a discipline and not a doctrine, it is, I think, Buddhism. There is, perhaps, no other world-religion which is so little concerned with metaphysical speculations as the religion of Buddha. It asks you to accept nothing that may not be established by pure psychological analysis, and that, consequently, may not be verified by ordinary human experience. And if its assertions are few and simple, its denials are fewer and very rarely positive. Buddhism has sometimes been characterised as agnostic. That there is a very strong note of agnosticism in the teachings of Buddha can hardly be denied. But it is an essentially healthy and reasonable kind of agnosticism. The type of agnosticism with which you and I are so familiar in this age, is as dogmatic in its denials of what it does not know as the orthodox Christian or Mahomedan or Hindu is in his assertions of what he professes to believe. The agnosticism of the Buddhist is not of this type. Its verdicts on the claims of other faiths is not that they are false, but simply that they are not-proven. And a credal religion that is characterised by this healthy mental attitude, and is peculiarly free from metaphysical speculations and unverifiable dogmas,—unverifiable, that is, by the ordinary processes of intellection,—must have, inspite of its creed, a very large element of true universalism in it. And all these peculiarities of the Buddhistic credalism that distinguish it from both Christian and Moslem credalism, is entirely due to its nativity. Buddhism is a child of Hinduism, and, therefore, has the dominant characteristics of its parent, namely, its spirit of toleration and universalism.

Hinduism—not a Creed but a Culture

Like Buddhism, Hinduism is also predominantly a discipline and a culture, and not at all a creed. The emphasis of Hinduism is not on what is known as faith in both Christianity and Islam, but what is called the path or *pantha* in Buddhism. The difference between Buddhism and Hinduism lies in the fact that while in Buddhism there is practically an absence of metaphysical speculations, Hinduism does not eliminate these speculations but tries, rather on the contrary, to seize and realise them as verified and verifiable facts and factors of the deepest spiritual life and experience. Buddhism is essentially agnostic. Hinduism is predominantly gnostic. But it is a gnosticism which does not repudiate and deny but fully accepts and transcends the fundamental facts of agnosticism. In fact, the note of Buddhistic agnosticism is derived from the rudimentary agnosticism of the earliest speculations of the Upanishads. In the Upanishads we have :—

> It (*i.e.*, the Ultimate Reality) is different from all that we know, and different also from all that we do not know. This is what we have heard from those teachers who explained that (Reality) to us.

And again :—

> Here (*i.e.*, in the attempt to know the Absolute), the injunction is that It is not this, It is not this.
>
> I do not say that I know it. I do not say that I do not know it. He who knows this truly knows.

These are all agnostic utterances. In these the Upanishads practically take up the same position which Buddhism subsequently took up. But while Buddhism stops with this fundamental agnosticism, Hinduism goes further. It says that the Absolute cannot be known in the way in which we know all that is known by us, that is, as *objects* of our knowledge, for to know the Absolute as such and through this method would be to destroy the very essence of the Absolute as the unrelated and the unconditioned. The things that we know are always conditioned by us as their knower. We are here the subject, and what we know are our object ; and the subject always conditions its object. The Absolute cannot be so conditioned. Consequently the Absolute cannot be known as *object*. But in knowing our object we also know ourselves as the subject. As subject we are not conditioned by our object but only condition it. The Absolute may be known, therefore, not as object but as subject, in the Self, through the Self, as the Self,—and even here our language, owing to its native limitations, is really symbolic ; for the prepositions, in, through, or as, implying duality and relation, do not apply to the Absolute and the Unrelated,—alone can the Absolute be realised. The final truth, therefore, is :—

"Shvetaketu, That (The Absolute or Brahman) art Thou".

Hindu Pantheism

Europe has labelled all this as Pantheism. And with the easy self-deception of all very clever people, Europe is satisfied in herself that by naming the thing it has fully explained all its mysteries. The popular idea of Pantheism is—everything is God, It is, therefore, regarded as the inevitable parent of Polytheism. And the conclusion is, on the face of it, absolutely irresistible. For, if everything be God, then there are as many gods as there are things. Pantheism and Polytheism are therefore only two sides of the same thing. But this popular interpretation of Pantheism is European, and not Indian. It is only when you accept the reality of what you call "everything,"—that is, the truth of the separate entities of these different things,—it is only upon this hypothesis, that you can establish Polytheism upon Pantheism. But the Hindu never accepted the reality of the phenomenal world. What the philosophers call the manifold of experience, has always been dismissed as unreal by Hindu speculations. To the Hindu both the "every-ness" and the "thing-ness," that is, both the isolation and the reality of what the European calls everything, are only apparent and not real, have truth and being only on the lower practical or *Vyavaharic* plane, as Samkara would say, but not on the plane of Reality or the *Paramarthic* plane, as he calls it. So you will see, that even the School of Absolute Monism in India does not understand by Pantheism what Christendom generally understands by that term.

What is the "Thou"

And the real reason of it is that the European has only known the word, but has rarely or never tried to seize the fundamental concept which the word conveys. The Hindu had fully seized that concept. And you too may seize it if you clearly analyse your own thought-life. When in answer to the query :—"What is Brahman or the Absolute ?"—the *Guru* replied, "Shvetaketu, That art thou," what is it that he referred to as "thou" in that answer ? It was not the body of Shvetaketu. The Hindu consciousness had, almost from pre-historic times, realised the distinction between the soul and the body. Neither could the teacher refer by "thou' to the intellect of Shvetaketu, for in Hindu psychology, the intellect is itself one of the senses, the eleventh sense. It is called *manas* in Sanskrit. The function of the *manas* is to seize the meaning of the senses, to distinguish one sensation from another, and thus to make knowledge of sensuous objects possible. The *manas* or the intellect lives and works in duality and difference. Neither is the "thou" the emotions or the will of Shvetaketu, for both our emotions and our will, like our intellect, live upon the sense of division and duality, and cannot therefore be the Absolute. And when our physical, our intellectual, our emotional and our volitional life,—all these are eliminated as not identical with the Absolute, then what else is it that remains in us ? Is there anything that is still left or not ? And if there is such a thing, what is it ? That is the real question. If we can discover that something, we may then know what it is that the *Guru* spoke of as "thou" when saying,—'Shvetaketu That (or the Absolute or Brahman) art thou."

"The Witness" in Us

Now, our senses, our intellect, our emotions and our will, all these are working perpetual changes in us. But we are always conscious of the fact that inspite of all these changes we are really one and the same. Indeed, unless we were the same in and through these constant changes, we could never have known even these very changes themselves. There must be something in us which bears witness unto all these changes. And the witness of a series of changes must be such as, though present in the changes, is not itself affected, that is changed, by them. Not one single experience of ours, whether sensuous or intellectual or emotional or volitional, is at all explicable except upon the hypothesis that there is this witness in us, which is changeless in the midst of changes, unrelated in the midst of relations, unconditioned in the midst of infinite conditions,—which is Eternal and Absolute. It is this thing in us, which constitutes our true Self, to which the *Guru* referred Shvetaketu when he said—"That art thou." In fact, if we only could detach ourselves from ourselves, free our consciousness from the false identification of our self with the changing sensations of our body, or the alternating consciousness and semi-consciousness and unconsciousness which is the condition of our intellectual life, or with the fitful flow of our emotions or the impulsions and repulsions of our will,—if we could detach our self from these, then we would at once see that in every act of knowledge, as well as in every movement of our affections and our will, we are constantly creating and cancelling the dualities through which these work, and are reaching out to that in us which is, really, the Absolute. Through this absolute self-detachment it is possible to reach the state in which all duality is cancelled, all differentiations cease, where there is neither object nor subject, neither knower nor known,—and therefore, no knowledge either, as we understand knowledge on the lower intellectual plane, but there is still Consciousness. We are perpetually reaching this consciousness, but are driven out of it immediately we get into it, by the outward movement of our senses and our intellect, our emotions and our will. But those who are called *yogees* in our literature, so discipline their senses, their mind, their emotions and their will, that these outward movements, natural to the senses, the intellect, the emotions and the will, are brought absolutely under control, and so these *yogees* can remain in this state of super-consciousness as long as they desire. It is those people only who know and truly understand what the *Guru* meant when he said, in reply to the disciple's question,—"What is Brahman ?"—"Shvetaketu, That art thou."

The Key to the Hindu Religion

And I am taking you through this dry and abstruse analysis, because it is here that you will find the real key to our religion. From what I have, very perfunctorily, stated above, you will see that even the most abstruse speculations of the Hindus are not mere speculations as speculation is understood in Europe. They are based upon positive inner experience, and are, therefore, as much verifiable through their specific methods as are the truths of what we claim in our day to be positive sciences.

The Scientific Character of Hinduism

In fact, I am not aware of any other world-religion which may claim to be so scientific as the religion of the Hindus. It is, I think, the only religion of an advanced type, that seeks absolute verification in actual experience of its most abstruse faiths and speculations. The Hindu wants nothing to be taken for granted, nay not even the universal theistic faith in a Supreme Being, who is the Author and Governor of the universe. Hinduism wants every man to rise to his own faith through his own efforts. The Hindu teacher, like the capable modern pedagogue, trained in the most advanced methods of pedagogy of our time, always tries to gently guide him to the truth, but never to forcibly impose his own ideas and opinions upon his pupil. This has been our orthodox method of spiritual training from very ancient times. And it is, therefore, that we have such endless diversities of faiths and practices in our religion, due to diversities of mental and spiritual endowments and acquisitions. This specific Hindu method of religious training is very lucidly illustrated in the story of Varuna and his son Bhrigu, recorded in the Taittiriya Upanishad.

The Bhrigu-Varuna Episode

Bhrigu, the son of the sage Varuna, so runs this story, one day went to his father and said, "Teach me, O revered one, the knowledge of Brahman." Varuna said :— "Seek to know Brahman through meditation." And with a view to help him to meditate properly, he indicated what Brahman is with this text :—

"That from which all that exist have come into being ; that by which after coming

> into being all that are, continue to be ; that towards which all objects move and into which all objects enter ;—know That as Brahman."

You will thus see that the teacher here does not present to his pupil his own conclusions regarding Brahman or the Ultimate Reality. He does not impose his own faith or idea upon him; but simply gives him a problem in equation, so to say, and wants him to solve it for himself. The Brahman is as yet unknown to the pupil. And the teacher keeps this character even in his own instruction. He speaks of Brahman here in the terms of what is called in Algebra, *X* and *Y*,—in the terms of the unknown. Only what he does to help his son and pupil is to place this unknown quantity, this *X* or *Y*, in relation to three known quantities, namely, birth, life and death. These are matters of universal experience. Things that were not, come to be ; this, in the case of living things, is called birth. Then things that come into being continue to be, this is life. Things that are, pass out of existence, this is what, in the case of humans and animals, we call death. These three things are matters of universal experience. Theist, atheist, agnostic, everybody has this three-fold experience. And Varuna here presents Brahman in relation to this universal experience. These are the known quantities of this equation. The unknown is Brahman. And Bhrigu was asked to find out the value of this unknown quantity, by meditation.

And he started his meditation with the analysis of these three universal experiences. And the first result that he got was that *Annam* (literally, Food) was Brahman. Food here really stands for the material basis of the universe. The conclusion that the Ultimate Reality is Food means really, in terms of the modern mind, that it is Matter. It is the final verdict of the physico-chemical group of the sciences. That "*Annam* is Brahman," is the universal verdict of materialism, both ancient and modern. Nay more, it is the highest generalisation of the group of experiences which are examined and analysed by the physical science. It is not an absolutely false conclusion either. Under certain mental conditions, however much we may pretend to do otherwise, we cannot by any means get beyond the material interpretation of experience. To those who are on this plane of intellectual and spiritual evolution, you can easily give, what to you are higher and fuller generalisations, as you may make a Christmas-present of a rich fur-coat to a friend, but can never create any real and living religious conviction. No amount of dogmatic instruction will be able to lift them out of these materialistic conclusions. They themselves must, with their own efforts, through further and deeper analysis of their own experience, and the fuller examination of their conclusions in the light of these new analyses and experiences, get out of these conclusions, however crude they may seem to others. And Varuna followed this rational method. When his son came and told him that he had found Brahman and that it was Food or *Annam*, he said again, as before: "By meditation seek to know Brahman."

The first conclusion that Varuna reached was that "Food is Brahman." By food he evidently meant the material basis of life. The phenomenon of birth with which he was familiar referred to the human, or at most to the animal kingdom. What we call Nature is apparently unborn and deathless. So Bhrigu started his analysis of experience with the familiar human kingdom. And here he saw that the foetus grows through the food taken by the mother during gestation. After birth, it is food again that maintains life. At death the body becomes the food of others. So he arrived at the conclusion that Food is Brahman. The form of it may be primitive and crude, but Bhrigu's first conclusion here regarding the Ultimate Reality is the universal conclusion, as I have already said, of all materialistic hypotheses of the universe. It is the conclusion of the physical sciences. Food here stands for matter. Having reached this conclusion, Bhrigu went to his father and said that he had found Brahman : Food is Brahman. The father said :—"By meditation seek to know Brahman."

Bhrigu went and commenced to meditate again. And now he started with an analysis of the first conclusion,—that Food is Brahman. Now, food is only for the living, and not for the dead. So it is life and not food, from which beings are born, by which beings are made to live, and finally it is another life that beings go to and enter. So he went and told his father : Life is Brahman. Even as we in our own time rise from the physical to the biological plane in our progressive analysis of experience, so did Bhrigu. And his conclusion was indeed, the universal conclusion of the biological group of the sciences. His father rejected this also, and said :—"By meditation seek to know Brahman."

So Bhrigu once again commenced to meditate, and rose in the next step from biology to psychology, from life or *prana* to *manas* or the sensorium, as the ultimate principle in creation. "*Manas* is Brahman," he went and told his father. His father said: "Seek to know Brahman by meditation." Bhrigu went to meditate again, and as a result of the analysis of the psychological explanation of experience, he found that what is called the Unity of Consciousness, which is the subject especially of philosophic speculation, is a higher principle. Psychology cannot explain itself without philosophy, as biology cannot explain itself without psychology, nor even physico-chemical sciences without biology. In this Unity of Consciousness, Bhrigu thought he found the solution of his problem. There was, however, one order of experience that had not been touched by any of the analyses so far made by Bhrigu. The Unity of Consciousness or *Bijnanam* as it is called in Sanskrit, explains as far as our intellectual life, but it cannot offer any rational ground or explanation of our emotional life. Least of all can it explain the *raison d'etre* of the phenomenal world. This he found, finally, in what he called *Anandam*, roughly rendered into English by joy or love.

"From *Anandam* have all things come into being, having come into being by *Anandam* are they kept alive, towards *Anandam* do they move and into *Anandam* do they enter."

Anandam is Brahman. This was the final conclusion at which Bhrigu arrived, as a result of these progressive analyses of experience.

I will not carry you through the further analysis to which the concept *Anandam* was subjected, and upon which the whole philosophy of the School of Love and Faith in Hinduism is based,

My main idea in citing this interesting old story here is to indicate what I have already described as the cultural character of the Hindu religion, as distinguished from the credal character of Christianity or Islam.

Hinduism—A Culture, not a Creed

The endless diversities of faith and rituals that are found in our religion, are entirely due to this cause. Modern pedagogy works upon the principle that the course and character of the training of every student must be determined by his or her individual endowments and tendencies, and consequently any attempt to bring all students under any one uniform system is fatal to true intellectual life and evolution. A healthy and rational system of education must study and recognise individual peculiarities and suit itself to these. Hinduism has always tried to follow this principle in regard to spiritual training and culture. Dogmas and creeds may to some extent be imposed from the outside, but real piety must grow from within. And what is to be developed from within must work upon the inner nature of the person in whom it is to grow. And as man's inner nature differs in the case of different people, so their religious duties and disciplines must also be different. What may be helpful to one person may not be helpful to another. There cannot be, therefore, any universal creed or any uniform ritual in a religion that seeks not to preach opinion but to grow character.

The Universal Reference of the Bhrigu-Varuna Episode

The story of Bhrigu however not only indicates the cultural character of Hinduism but has, it seems to me, a much wider reference and meaning. Bhrigu here may well stand for the whole humanity. And the way in which he rose gradually from one conclusion to another in his search after God or the Absolute, may well be taken as presenting the complete history of the evolution of religion. His first conclusion, as I have already told you, is the universal conclusion of Materialism. This Materialism is not a special product of our age. Modern science is not the real parent of it either. Our scientific investigations and discoveries have added certain new forms to the materialistic interpretation of the universe, but the spirit that stands behind it is as old as the human race. Indeed, as we see in the story of Bhrigu, it is the earliest result of the application of the opening intelligence of man to the solution of the problem of the universe. It took, God alone knows how many milleniums, for man to see anything beyond what his senses revealed. And the senses never can of themselves take us farther than what Bhrigu called *Annam* or Food. Of course, the senses themselves loudly repudiate their pretensions to any form of finality. They seem to be perpetually crying, as much in our rational life, through the intellect, as in our emotional life, through the unquenchable thirst of our heart, that they are not an end unto themselves. But who hears their ceaseless warnings ? It needs long and tedious disciplines to hear what the senses are always telling us. It took thousands of years for man to catch the first faintest note of this constant warning. And even now he has heard only a mere echo of it. And as long as we are completely under the spell of the senses, so long the only possible realisation of the Absolute by us must be in the form in which Bhrigu realised it. We may not call it after him *Annam* but Electron, not Food but Force. But by whatever name called the reality is the same. In fact, it can hardly be denied that one of the most patent results of our modern scientific achievements have been to quicken the powers of our senses both by natural and artificial means, and thereby to extend our sensuous hold on the universe. And in proportion as we extend our sense-domination over phenomena, in that proportion our sense-life also extends and strengthens its dominion over us. Our servants, thus, always become our masters. Modern science instead of weakening, has therefore visibly strengthened the hold of the material world over our mind. And one of the signs of this renewed domination of matter over mind in our age, is seen in the increasing materialisation of our old spiritual concepts. Both in England and America there has grown up in course of the last quarter of a century a new group of terms that seeks to express the profoundest experiences of our inner life in the technique of the physical sciences. And in view of this increasing materialisation of our thoughts, how can we possibly reach out to the profound mysteries of the spiritual life unless it be through mere material concepts? The Hindu has always recognised the impossibility of transcending the limitations of our nature except through following the inner bents and trends of that nature itself. Those who are completely under the domination of the sensuous can rise gradually to the consciousness of the spiritual only through these very senses themselves. The senses must, by some means or other, be supernaturalised for them. It is through this supernaturalisation of the senses that these people can gradually rise to the faith in the supersensuous. This is the secret of the so-called idolatry of the Hindus. It is, of course, only one of the aspects of this complex culture. It has many other aspects, of which I shall speak D. V.—later on. The Hindu's so-called worship of stocks and stones has been admittedly ordained for this purpose, namely, to lead him through the senses to the contemplation of the supersensuous. And what these so-called stocks and stones do for the ordinary Hindu, occultism and spiritism are seeking to do for the modern European and American. Occultism and spiritism, whatever may or may not be be the exact measure of truth in these, mean really the manifestation of spiritual phenomena on the physical plane and the interpretation of the supersensuous in the terms of the senses. Those who have truly risen to the vision of the spiritual do not need these signs and wonders to create or confirm their faith in the unseen. But these signs and wonders are however needed to create and confirm the faith of those who lack real spiritual acquisitions. The same thing is true of the ordinary Hindu worshipper also. He is still completely under the domination of his senses. The first thing to do for him, to create a sense of the supersensuous, is to gradually train his mind to habits of detachment from the sensuous. And these habits are cultivated by two means. One of these is to establish the domination of the will over the impulses and activities of the senses ; and the other is to train the mind to see the Unseen in the seen.

Physical Purity : Cleanliness

The first of these is called in the literature of Hinduism, *deha-shuddhi*. *Deha* means the body, and *shuddhi* purification. The purification of the body is the first step in Hindu spiritual culture. The Hindu had realised, ages and ages before the modern man, the close and organic interdependence between our body and our mind. Physiological psychology, almost a new discovery in modern Europe, has been a very old science in this country. And it is because the Hindu had fully realised the organic dependence of our mind and morals upon the state of our body, aud more particularly upon that of our nerves, that he has always insisted upon a course of psycho-physical disciplines and practices as an absolute condition-precedent to the growth of morals as well as of the true spiritual life. *Deha-shuddhi* or purification of the body is the common name of this course of psycho-physical disciplines. Personal cleanliness, characteristic of the Hindu, is the fruit of these age-long disciplines. The Hindu is therefore admittedly the most clean animal in the human kingdom. This cleanliness means not only that he is a much-washed animal but that he observes most punctilliously this law of cleanliness in whatever he does. If the Hindu touches his own lips with his hand, the hand becomes impure. and he cannot touch anything, neither food nor raiment, without carefully and completely washing that hand. The clothes that he puts on while going to the outer world, whether it be the court or the market or the house of a friend even, cannot strictly speaking be taken back into the living rooms of his house until they are thoroughly washed and dried. For cleanliness a Hindu's house has always the sanctified odour of a temple. The Englishman's house, they say, is his castle ; the Hindu's house, my child, is his temple. It is holy ground. So like Moses he always takes off his shoes when he enters its precincts. Like his person, his food also must always be religiously clean. The Hindu's ideal of cleanliness has apparently a lot to do with the restrictions imposed by his religion in the matter of both food and drink. There are Hindus to whom all manner of animal food is prohibited. But even those to whom these restrictions have not been extended, are not allowed to take every kind of meat. The deer is regarded as the purest of animal. Consequently venison is the most approved meat. Pork is absolutely prohibited owing to the character of the swine. But the same objection does not apply to the wild boar, against which therefore there is no such rigid restriction. The Bengali Hindu is not allowed to take domestic fowls, but the wild species is not prohibited. So in regard to fishes also, those of observed unclean habits are avoided. The prohibition of beef. as well as of the meat of the females of all animals, is due to other causes. The prohibition of fermented drinks is also partly due to considerations of cleanliness. Many of our domestic habits and social usages had their origin in this religious regard of the Hindu for the quality of cleanliness. The pious Hindu takes his meals not out of porcelain or metallic plates but out of banana-leaves that may be thrown away every time they are used. On festive occasions, when guests are invited by scorces and hundreds, the use of the banana-leaves for plates is universal, not merely because of the difficulty of providing so many plates, but for the graver reason that when a person eats out of a metallic plate, it becomes impure, and can only be purified by burning it in a forge. The Hindu seems to have always known it that many an infectious disease passes from one person to another through the excretions of the mouth. The sputum has always been regarded by him almost as impure as the excreta. He never tolerated therefore in his social intercourse the civilised practice of osculation. The crusade against osculation as a prolific medium of many diseases just started in Europe and America, was therefore never needed in India.

These disciplines of cleanliness have however not merely a physical or hygienic value but have always been regarded by the Hindu as necessary for his religious and spiritual life also. Modern civilisation has long treated these disciplines as survivals of old-world superstitions. It is however to be hoped that the progress of psycho-physical and psychological researches and the consequent recognition of the organic interdependence of our mind and our body will gradually lead even the civilised man to understand and appreciate the ethical reference of the physical disciplines of Hinduism.

"Instructive" and "Constructive"

This ethical reference of the apparently external and physical disciplines of Hinduism has scarcely been recognised by the European or American student of our life and institutions. Even our own modern-educated classes have frequently found it difficult to do so. The inevitable formalism of the essentially forensic character of Christian ethics is largely responsible for this misunderstanding. An excessive emphasis on the dogma of the freedom of the human will on the one hand, and a more or less complete ignorance of the organic interdependence between our nerves and the inhibitive powers of our will on the other, have combined to create this formalism, and to make Christian ethics predominantly instructive. Like the Christian religion, Christian morals also are propagated through the usual missionary method of preaching or instruction. You have therefore ethical text-books and elaborately-equipped Sunday Schools for inparting moral instructions to the young all over Europe and America. The Christian pulpit tries to do the same work for adults and elders of the community. What the Sunday School teacher or the Christian minister does is simply to proclaim what is right and should be done, and then practically to leave the duty of doing the right to the individuals concerned. If they are able to do so, they receive their due meed of approbation and praise; if they fail they receive the condemnation and punishment which are their due. Everything, you will thus see, is practically left in the matter of the right regulation of conduct, to the chances of individual effort and strength. Christian ethics has so far taken little notice of the constitutional capacities or incapacities of individuals in regard to the ethical life. Differences of physical or intellectual eudowments are recognised, and, where necessary, generously condoned. But Christendom has not as yet given almost any recognition to original moral endowments. It is only very recently that Lombroso and the school of criminal anthropology of which he was the father, have discovered the congenital character of the criminal propensities of at least a certain class of instinctive criminals. These propensities are constitutional and organic and cannot be cured without a change in the organism itself. Hindu psychology had recognised from of old this organic character of man's moral aptitudes and virtuous impulses. It has always recognised the fact that both our real intellectual and our true moral life are largely established upon our nervous system. Differences of personal temperamants,– one is phlegmatic and another impassioned, one is hard to irritate and another quick to resent, one is excessively sensitive to sex-impulse and another almost impervious to it, one is selfish another generous, one is cringy another free-handed,—all these are constitutional, and are related to very subtle differences in different nerve-structures. Fully recognising these facts of common experience, the Hindu has always been naturally slow to condemn and punish and ready to condone and forgive the wrong-doer. The forensic formalism of Christian ethics has developed a somewhat keener sense of personal responsibility in the European than what is usually seen in the Indian. The psychological realism of Hindu ethics has to a large extent prevented the growth of any strong sense of moral responsibility in the Indian. On the other hand, his keen sense of personal responsibility has made the European impatient of people's weaknesses and intolerant of their misdeeds; while the general weakness of this sense in the Hindu has made him divinely patient of people's faults and foibles, and uniformly tolerant of all human wrongs. The soul of ethics in the Hindu character is therefore not what is called the conscience in Christian literature, but rather love. And the real basis of it is our nerve-organisation.

The Ethics of Psycho-Physics

Hindu ethics has always fully recognised this fact. Psycho-physical disciplines have, therefore, formed so fundamental a part of the moral and religious training of the Hindu. The purification of *deha* or the physical body, called also *bhuta-suddhi* in Sanskrit, of which I have just spoken, formed therefore the very first step in this training. The daily baths and ablutions as well as the various restrictions regarding food and drink have an admitted psycho-physical reference. All food is divided in our books into three classes : the highest of these is that which is recommended to the Brahmins, those whose special function is to lead and shape the soul-life of the people. They must themselves be supremely spiritual. And the proper food for the spiritually minded people is, that which is sweet, and fatty (has vegetable fat in it), and substantial and pleasant to take. This is the class of food that contributes to health and strength, happiness and long life and vigour and virility. The next class of food consists of things that are bitter, acid, have too much salt, is too warm or dry or pungent or hot. This is the class of food that is proper for the warrior class ; it causes pain and trains one to suffer pain and sorrow or bereavement. That which has stood overnight, the flavour natural to which is lost, which is decomposed, or consists of the leavings of other people's plates, or which is forbidden to be used in sacrifices ; these are the last class of food. This class of food contributes to inertia and animalism, and is liked only by those whose nature is essentially very low and vicious. The Hindu realised that what we eat or drink has a very great influence upon the condition of our inner life. Certain kinds of food inevitably quicken our animalities. That drinks of a certain class do this is universally recognised even by the modern man. Why cannot then our foods have also the same effect? Meat, for instance, produces certain inner tendencies that are not produced by pure vegetables. I remember one of your publicists proclaiming some years ago that the superiority of the European, as a fighting animal over the non-European, was largely, if not entirely, due to the beef-and-beer consuming capacity of the former. Though for many many centuries past the Hindu has prohibited beef, it will be interesting to you to be told that both meat and strong drinks have always been freely permitted by the Hindu scriptures to those whose special function in the social organism has been to fight and rule. Our restrictions regarding food and drink have thus far more than a mere physical or hygienic reference.

In fact, to fully understnd, even where it may not be possible for the modern consciousness to fully support, the complicated restrictions enjoined upon the Hindu in regard to what is called inter-dining, we must view these in the light of Hindu psycho-physics. The conclusions of this science as the Hindu understood and investigated it, may have to be largely modified by the large experiences and investigations of our day, but we cannot entirely ignore the fundamental basis of these restrictions. The Hindu refuses to eat food cooked by certain classes. The original reason of this prohibition was absolutely psycho-physical. These classes were at one time really unclean in their habits and very low in their manner of living. They made no discrimination between foods and drinks,—between those that were likely to be conducive, and those that were likely to be prejudicial, to the higher life. In fact, even in our own day most of these classes or castes, are more or less careless in regard to personal cleanliness. They scarcely observe the almost universal Hindu rule concerning the contamination of food and drink through contact with what is called in Sanskrit, *uchhistam*, or what has been left after eating or drinking by others. These are people who eat out of each other's plates or drink out of each other's glass, or who, in other ways are not very particular about the contact, either direct or remote, of foodstuffs with the sputum of people. These are people who eat all kinds of forbidden foods and indulge in all kinds of prohibited drinks. But the Hindu believes, whether rightly or wrongly, that it is not merely the sputum of people that contaminates food and drink, but even their very breath, which carries with it microscopic particles of their inner organs, is also a source of such contamination, especially when it comes through the mouth. It is, therefore, that you will see, in truly orthodox Hindu households, the cook, even though a man or woman of the highest caste, ties a piece of clean cloth over the lips to prevent the breath coming even into the suspicion of any contact with the dishes cooked by him or her. These restrictions, though carried like many things else, by our people to what may seem irrational excesses, have, however, this psycho-physical reference. These do not, however, mean in any sense whatever, any hatred of the classes with regard to whom they have to be observed. In fact, these restrictions apply under certain circumstances even to the members of one's own family. In every orthodox Hindu family, not even the mistress or the daughter of the house is permitted to enter the kitchen or touch any food or drink without having previously bathed and changed her usual clothings. And it is because these rules regarding personal cleanliness were not strictly observed by every class or caste that taking food from those who did not observe them, was prohibited to those who did.

Indeed, it seems clear from our ancient records that at one time these restrictions did not at all apply as between one higher caste and another. The Brahmins used at one time to freely partake of food cooked by the Kshatriyas, for instance ; and the prohibition did not apply, I think, even to the Vaisyas. All these three were called the twice-born castes. The laws of personal cleanliness were the same among all these three castes. And, consequently, there was no objection to their dining with one another. These restrictions came in much later, when, I think, the neighbouring non-Aryan communities commenced to be taken into the Aryan fold, and with this expansion there entered a large variety of different stocks with different habits and customs, into the common Aryan society. Be that however as it may, all these outer physical or physiological restrictions and disciplines have, in the eye of the Hindu, a distinct ethical value. The Hindu believes in the organic character of the ethical life. It is by no means so absolutely self-determined as it is generally regarded by many people. The Bhagavad-Geeta says, as you may perhaps remember, that the actual agent of what we claim as our acts is not one, but five, and these five agents are responsible for everything we do. These are :—(i) our body, (ii) our self or the empirical ego as the philosophers would say, (iii) our senses, (iv) the multifarious efforts that we make to realise our purpose, and (v) the impulse of the Divine. All our acts are the joint product of these. And this being so, it is sinful perversity, says the Geeta, to look upon the self as the only agent.

Moral Education

True moral education therefore, the Hindu says must involve the training and regulation of all these five agencies that combine and co-operate with one another to originate all our activities and work up our conduct in life. The relation between these five agencies is rather one of co-ordination than that of subordination of some to the domination of others. In the higher stages of evolution, the more spiritual of these agencies do control the less spiritual, it is true ; and at last, the self, freed by long course of disciplines from the bondage of the senses and all their outer stimuli, can and do exercise almost complete sovereignty over them. But this stage is reached when the education of the self is completed, and not when it is only started or is progressing. As long as this high stage is not reached, our body and our senses, our intellect, our emotions and our will, and the outer stimuli that are constantly quickening these, all act and react upon one another, and it is impossible to control and regulate any one of these five-fold agencies that are jointly responsible for our moral life, without simultaneously controlling and regulating the others. And it should be recognised that these various agencies have a certain measure of what may be called local autonomy, each within its own proper sphere. The body and the senses, for instance, have this autonomy within the limits of the physical and the sense-life. No one can, therefore, neglect the laws of physiology or psycho-physics, and yet expect, by sheer exercise of the will, to control their inner propensities or their outer actions. Is it not absolute folly, my child, to demand a sort of anarchist freedom in the matter of what one shall eat or drink, or what life one shall lead, in regard to one's physical or sense-activities, and at the same time hope to attain the highest ethical ends ? Those who cherish these fancies, either do not know or do not bear it in mind, that our foods and drinks, our associations and conversations, our works and our recreations, all these are constantly helping or hindering the growth of healthy nerve-tissues, which form really the very plinth and foundation of our moral life. And it is in the light of these that we must study and understand the complex outer ordinances and regulations of the religious life of the Hindu. There may possibly be many errors of observation in the system of Hindu psycho-physics, upon which these externalities of the Hindu's religion are based. The more thorough and scientific investigations of our age may discover these errors and remove them. But these are matters of detail, which do not in the least destroy the fundamental Hindu position that true moral education must be essentially constructive and not merely instructive as it as predominantly in Christendom. And the more you know and understand the Hindu system of ethics, the more, I think, my child, you will see the need of largely amending the fundamentally forensic formalism of what proudly proclaims itself as high and superior Christian ethics. In fact, the close psycho-physical reference of ethical culture is not entirely unknown even to Christian or Moslem experiences either. Indeed, the psycho-physical disciplines of Hinduism are not exclusively Hindu. Almost all the old-world religions had them. We find these in Judaism. They were fully recognised as essential to the higher religious and spiritual culture by the Catholic church. They are found in Islam. The main difference in regard to this matter between Hinduism on the one side, and Christianity or Islam on the other, lies in this, namely, that while in the former these are enjoined upon all or almost all classes, in the latter systems they are almost entirely confined to the higher cultures of the saints and devotees. In other words, that which has been organised into social and socio-religious institutions among us, exists only as special disciplines for the monks and dervishes, in the Christian or the Moslem world.

The Education Of The Will

There is, however, another aspect of these socio-religious disciplines of Hinduism, which also should be carefully considered. The injunctions and prohibitions of Hinduism, in regard to the utmost outer concerns of man's life, have a very salutary effect upon his character by helping to strengthen the inhibitive powers of the will, as well as by training the individual to perpetually give preference in his daily works and recreations to the good over the pleasant. The range of what is usually called personal freedom in Christendom, but which practically means so often the range of the unrestrained use and indulgence of the senses, is almost infinitely more limited in the socio-religious life of the Hindu than in that of the Christian, especially of the advanced Protestant, and more especially of the conscientious Non-Conformist. Even what are regarded as absolutely legitimate enjoyments of the senses by our Christian or Mahomedan friends, are hedged in, by the socio-religious laws of the Hindus, by numerous restrictions. Not only there are certain kinds of food absolutely prohibited, but even where a particular class of edibles are not so tabooed, there even the use of these is forbidden on particular days of the lunar month. Certain vegetables, for instance, are forbidden in certain *tithis* or phases of the moon. On the face of it, this class of restrictions seems to be utterly irrational. But if you look at these from the view-point of real ethical training, namely, as exercise in self-control, I think, even we, who are so steeped in the spirit of what so proudly proclaims itself as modern rational life, shall have to concede some ethical value to them. The Bengalee Hindu who is allowed to take meat, cannot kill an animal, strictly speaking, for his own delectation. It is the meat of animals that have been duly sacrificed which alone is permissible, and not butcher's meat. And is it possible even for the most conceited rationalist to deny the salutariness of this restriction ? It works in a two-fold way : the animal that is to be sacrificed, must in the first place be absolutely clean and healthy. You cannot sacrifice lean and worn-out or diseased and dying animals, and then partake of its meat. In the next place, there are special places or particular occasions, and appointed hours which you cannot create, when alone can these sacrifices be held. And all these help to curb and control your desire for animal food even when your religion may not altogether prohibit it. As in the matter of our palate, so also in regard to the other senses. The Hindu has always recognised that the desire for food and for procreation are the two strongest sense-impulses in humanity. And consequently he has hedged in even the perfectly legitimate satisfaction of both these impulses by the most minute restrictions. St. Paul fully realised the importance of these restraints in regard to the sex-relation, when he said that even the married shall live as if they were unmarried. The Hindu did not leave so vital a matter affecting as much the life of the individual as of the society of which he may be a member, to be guided merely by the moral sense or the inhibitive power of the will of the individual. Working within the general limitations of the marital relation, he has ordained numerous laws and restrictions to secure the healthy exercise of this vital function, calculated to simultaneously secure the health of both the individual and the race. The Hindu who has not been liberalised from the bondage of his national religion and superstitions, still lives for more than half the days of each month, in obedience to these injunctions, even when he is married, as if he were unmarried. It is for this reason, that the modern civilised problem of what the American press was so keenly discussing some years ago, as the problem of prostitution in married life, is as yet an unknown problem among us, except possibly, in a very insignificant section of those who have commenced to be civilised after the European model. It is, of course, a rather new problem even in the West, which owes its origin to the general decadence of Christian faith and the decline of the old influence of healthy Christian disciplines over the life of the modern man in Christendom. You will thus see that in the socio-religious life of the Hindu there is a much narrower range for the indulgence of the senses and the appetites than there is, perhaps, in any other system. The Hindu has to submit to much greater restraints even in what are regarded as quite legitimate enjoyments everywhere than the votaries of the other great world-religions. Not only are there numerous fast days in every month, but on the day previous to every domestic celebration, the master of the family has to fast partially and abstain from even the permissible enjoyments of life. The Hindu celebrates the anniversary of the death of his parents and of his grand-parents also as a sacred religious ceremony. And he has to observe both the day of the ceremony as well as that preceding it, as sacred days, when he must abstain from all manner of sense-enjoyments whether in regard to food and drink or other matters, and devote the whole time to the contemplation of the higher life. On these days he must not take his ordinary meals or his usual food ; must not be engaged in games of any kind ; must not speak harsh words to any one, or indulge even in legitimate conjugal association, or in any other way give the least latitude to his senses, and appetites. There are numerous days in the year dedicated to different gods and goddesses, and those who worship them, have to observe similar disciplines on these occasions. It is by these means that the general socio-religious schemes of the Hindus help materially to advance the real ethical life of the people. It is to these that we owe all the humanity of our national character. Our proverbial patience and mildness, our admitted respect for all life, both human and non-human ; our special spiritual aptitudes, and our general freedom from some of the most obtrusive vices of civilised humanity ; all these are largely due to these socio-religious institutions and the physico-ethical disciplines associated with them, which are so often dismissed by the modern man both in Europe and even in India, as mere superstitions.

Mastery Over Nature

And the fundamental object of all these

restraints and regulations is to train the mind to habits of self-control and self-detachment, and, thereby, to free it from the universal bondage of Nature. Strictly speaking, the attainment of an absolute mastery over Nature is the central idea of all these disciplines. The European also is anxious for the attainment of this mastery. All the superior claims of modern European civilisation over older civilisations of the world, are based upon the wonderful mastery that Europe thinks she has been able to establish over Nature through her advanced scientific attainments. That, of course, is a kind of mastery, no doubt. But frankly speaking, my child, it has often seemed to me like the mastery of the valet over his own lord and master. The valet studies the weak points of his master, and exercises immense control over him through these weaknesses. Is not Europe's control over Nature, very largely of this character ? Europe has been investigating the laws of Nature, has been discovering the secrets through which Nature works in her own dominions ; and by operating upon Nature through these secrets, Europe is compelling Nature to serve the increasingly expansive material ends of her children. But the process, however clever and commendable, does not at all touch even the outermost fringe of the fundamental problem that man's intimate relations with outer Nature creates. Indeed, Europe seems to have almost completely lost the very consciousness of that fundamental problem. And because Europe has practically lost sight of it, she is heaping problems upon problems, and complications upon complications, in her march of progress, without being able to even remotely suggest any remedy or solution for these. Scientific conquest of Nature has immensely increased naterial wealth in Europe. And this increased material prosperity has enormously increased the material wants of her children also ; but has it advanced their manhood, or even their happiness ? In seeking to establish a larger and larger mastery over Nature through the advancement of the Natural Sciences, has not Europe been increasingly losing her own self-mastery ? Indeed, this proud conquest of outer Nature has, it seems to me, its compensation in a corresponding conquest of the soul of man by his senses.

The Hindu had analysed his relations with outer Nature more thoroughly than what the European has perhaps as yet done. The Hindu saw that Nature's hold upon him was only through his senses and his appetites. Here, in his sense-life, lay the root of the cruel domination of Nature over man. The way of Science, such as is being so diligently followed in Europe, is really not to curtail but continually to extend and strengthen the dominion of outer Nature over man's sense-life. The practical application of the laws of science for removing human want, means increased satisfaction of the senses. And this increased service of the senses increases inevitably the hold over man, of what is called "the world, the flesh, and devil," in your popular parlance. And these increased demands of the senses upon the attention and activities of man, mean not the diminution but rather a corresponding increase of Narure's true mastery over us. The Hindu knew all this ; and, therefore, he did not follow this suicidal plan in the evolution of his culture and civilisation. In the face of his ancient records it is not possible to argue that he never tried to study and discover the secrets of Nature. Dr. Prafulla Chandra Ray's recent publication, the History of Hindu Chemistry, and especially Principal Brajendra Nath Seal's Introduction, published in the second volume of this monumental work, which has been accepted universally as the highest authority on the subject even in Europe, furnish convincing evidence of what the Hindu had achieved in the domain of the physical sciences ages before Bacon. But the spiritual genius of the Hindu clearly saw that the real mastery of man over Nature does not lie that way. The root of our serfdom to Nature is not in Nature's strength but in our own weaknesses. It is through our senses that Nature exercises her cruel sway over us. And, consequently, if we could only control these senses, if we could so train our body and our senses that these would be absolutely impervious to the influences of the forces of outer Nature, then we could easily gain a mastery over these outer things which would be permanent and absolute.

This complete mastery has been the aim and objective of all the psycho-physical disciplines of the Hindu of which I have been speaking. The entire system of our *yogic* disciplines has this mastery for its primary end. It is through these disciplines that the Hindu *yogee* is able to attain that perfect physical state in which neither heat nor cold can affect him in the least. The ordinary physiological functions of their bodies are, therefore, always under the complete control of these *yogees.* They can go without both food and drink, as well as without sleep or rest for long periods without suffering any discomfort or ill-health. There are *yogees* who have so trained their bodies that even the vital functions of the lungs and the heart may be stopped by them at their will, without loss of health or life. Of course, the number of such adepts is not large. Even all our holy men do not attain these physical lordships. Many of them, especially those who follow the way of Love and Faith, do not even care for these powers. But still there are such men even to-day, whose powers in these respects have been seen and testified to by even men with modern scientific education in the country.

A *yogee* of this type, is a well-known personality in West Bengal. He lives in the sacred town of Baidyanath, on the East Indian Railway. Two well-known medical gentlemen of Calcutta saw him some time back ; and they have borne witness unto the wonderful mastery that this Hindu *yogee* has over all the limbs and organs of his body. He can move all the muscles of his stomach at his will, and clear his bowels by this means far more completely than can be done by any known purgative. This was actually seen and tested by these medical gentlemen In the presence of these gentlemen this saintly *yogee* suspended for a time not only the functions of the lungs but even of the heart, and stayed in this state of suspended animation for a length of time which is inexplicable by modern science.

I do not want you to attach any occult significance to these powers. Indeed, the *yogees* themselves, when they are true and genuine, strongly condemn any such interpretation or assessment. They look upon these physical or psycho-physical acquisitions not as the end of their culture but only as mere by-products. They do not seek these, they come of themselves It is, however, with these powers that the first step in the progress of the soul towards real and true salvation, is taken. For if the body and the senses are not so completely brought under control that no change of outer natural conditions shall in the least affect them, how then can you expect to concentrate your mind absolutely in the contemplation of the Supreme ? And it is as a preliminary preparation for the attainment of this concentration, that these physical and psycho-physical disciplines have their real spiritual value. The true end and objective of these psycho-physical disciplines is to acquire a complete detachment of the soul from its physical and psysiological habiliment.

Idolatry Or Idea-latry

If the main object of all the socio-religious and psycho-physical regulations and disciplines of Hinduism has always been to train the self to completely detach itself from its accidental, though for the time being organic, connections with its outer physical and physiological habitat ; that of all our apparently sensuous and external religious ritualism has been to train the mind to see and seize the Unseen in and through the seen. The outsider, looking upon these rituals in the light of his own special religious traditions and beliefs, or in that of his narrow generalisations from the study of what he calls Primitive Culture, has frequently characterised and condemned these popular Hindu rituals as idolatry. He has placed, thus, the Hindu's image-worship, in the same class as what is called by European scholars totemism and animism. These popular rituals have also been denounced from time to time even by our own teachers as ignorant and carnal. They have admittedly the evils of all ceremonialism. They have an undoubted tendency to create a divorce between the form and the spirit of higher religious culture. But yet, it is absolutely untrue and unjust to place this so-called idolatry of the Hindu on the same level of intellectual or spiritual evolution as the sacrifices and rituals of primitive man. Those who do so forget that this so-called idolatry of the Hindus came in at a much later stage of the religious evolution of the Hindu people than that at which the so-called totemism or animism of primitive culture is found in history.

And to understand this difference between what is called the idolatry of the Hindus and the idolatry of primitive culture, you have simply to obseve the particular course of religious evolution in India. You may possibly know that one of your own thinkers, the late Professor Caird, in his Evolution of Religion, mentions the principal stages of it as (i) Objective, (ii) Subjective and (iii) Universal. Personally, I strongly object to these terms, as exceedingly misleading. But this is not the occasion nor the place to enter into that large discussion. I would prefer to name these three phases of the general history and scheme of the evolution of religion, as (i) Perceptive, (ii) Reflective, and (iii) Imaginative. Religion originates with man's contact and conflict with what may best be called his not-me. We call this not-me in Sanskrit *idam*, in contradistinction to the me or *aham*, as it is called in our language. These are the two primal and universal categories according to Hindu thought. All the universe comes under either the one or the other of these two categories. They are present in consciousness even at the lowest stage of our mental evolution. In the earliest stage, this not-me is an object of the senses. Man sees it, hears it, touches it, tastes it, seizes it with his outer senses. The earliest gods everywhere are, therefore, sense-objects. You find evidence of it as much in your own Old

Testament as you do in our own Vedas. You find it in the recorded religious experiences both of Rome and Greece. It is universally acknowledged that the present record of the Old Testament is the product of a later and much advanced redaction, representing a much more advanced stage of the evolution of Hebrew thought than what the original documents referred to. But still there are the clearest possible evidences of what may be called a perceptive God-consciousness both in the Book of Genesis and in the Exodus. All the prominent gods of the Vedas are cognised by the senses. Varuna, like Uranus, is the visible sky-god. The omniscience of Varuna is clearly due to the fact,—cognised by the senses—that the sky above us holds all, overlooks all, enters into all, whether great or small, whether far or near. If time and space had permitted, I would have cited detailed evidence of this universal perceptive character of early religion. The Prophetic Books of the Old Testament, our own Upanishads, the philosophical interpretations of Greek Mythology, all these represent the reflective stage of religious evolution. It is essentially a protestant and antithetical stage. It is characterised by a universal tendency towards mental and metaphysical abstractions. This antithesis does not however hold the mind of man for long. The intellect becomes restless under the confused conflict between idealities and actualities, between the abstractions of thought and the concrete realities of outer experiences, between the unseen and the seen. It is then that religious imagination steps into the breach and with the help of a superb process of idealisation and spiritualisation commences to work up a reconciliation between the unseen and the seen.

In our own Upanishads there are two distinct classes of worship. One of these is called *Byetirekee Upasana.* It means the adoration of the Supreme by the method of exclusion or abstraction. The worshipper here tries to meditate on the Deity by constantly saying,—"He is not this : He is not this." In other words, he tries to think of God as absolutely different and standing away from all that is cognised by the senses or can even be concieved in thought. This is the method of worshipping, if worship it may at all be called, the Nirguna Brahman or the Abstract Universal. The other method is called *Anvayee Upasana.* It means the adoration of the Supreme not by abstracting Him from sense-realities but by seeking to seize and realise Him in and through these very realities. In this method the text is—"All this phenomenal universe is filled by

Brahman." It is the method of idealisation and spiritualisation. Here the Supreme, though unseen, is yet the very *esse* and *posse* of the seen. The eys sees Him not, but yet it sees all that is seen because He is the very eye of the eye. So with all the other senses. He is the ear of the ear, the mind of the mind, the life of life. Himself without the senses He is yet the very soul and essence of both the senses and their objects. He not only transcends all but is equally immanent in all.

This immanental conception of the Absolute forms the very plinth and foundation of the third and the most advanced stage of religious evolution. Religious Imagination, characteristic of this stage, works upon this philosophy of Divine Immanence. What is ignorantly called the idolatry of the Hindus, belongs not to the primitive perceptive stage, to which the so-called totemism and animism of primitive culture belong, but to the third or the imaginative stage of religious evolution. It is really not idolatry at all but idealatry.

In judging of this so-called idolatry of the Hindus we must not forget one very important fact, namely, that this idolatry was introduced after the general philosophy of the Upanishads had permeated the entire thought and culture of the people. The gods and goddesses of present-day Hindu ceremonials are not really Vedic. None of the ancient Vedic gods, neither Indra nor Varuna nor the heavenly twins, the Asvini-kumaras, nor any of the old gods are objects of popular worship now. Though the terms, Durga, Kalee, Sarasvatee etc. occur in the Vedas, they are not the names of goddesses, not at least of those who are worshipped now under these names. All these gods and goddesses belong not to the Vedas but to the Puranas. And in the Puranas, we have most decidedly the later records of what I have described as the imaginative stage of religious evolution. This is one of the main reasons why these gods and goddesses should be regarded not as idols, but as what may be called 'ideas', not gross meterial images but refined spiritual imageries.

Gods and Goddesses as Superior Spiritual Beings

This is one interpretation of this so-called idolatry. There is, however, another and more orthodox interpretation also. According to this interpretation, these gods and goddesses are not mere ideas or imageries but real beings infinitely more spiritual and powerful than the humans and differing from them only in degree and not in kind. These gods belong to another and a higher sphere of being. They can exercise as potent a control over the destinies of men even as men can over those of the lower animal world. They are immortals, but not equal to the Supreme, who rules them as much as He rules mankind. Though much purer than humans, these gods have the same passions and are as much subject to anger and jealousy and other spiritual deficiencies as men and women. Their grace can, therefore, be sought by due offerings. And it is to secure the favour of these superior intelligences for the furtherance of more or less mundane ends that these gods and goddesses are usually worshipped. It is very remarkable, indeed, that in the texts used in the worship of these gods and goddesses very rarely have we any reference to the highest spiritual life. The prayers offered to them are mostly for progeny and wealth and honour and victory over one's enemies. This is the usual prayer in the current liturgy for the worship of Kalee, Durga and the other manifestations of Shakti.

I have already told you something of this Shakti cult. Though many people worship Shakti as a goddess among many gods and goddesses, there are some Shakta worshippers, who interpret Her as *Prakriti*, and whose worship of Shakti belongs altogether to a very different and spiritually higher category. This

Shakti, by whatever name called, whether Kalee or Durga or Jagaddhatree, or Bhavanee—and these are only different names of the one and the same Reality,—represents, as I already said in my last letter, the eternally self-differentiated Being of the Absolute. It is the same Reality as the Christian Logos, which was in the beginning with God, and which is God, the very God of God. To these advanced devotees the worship of Shakti is no more idolatrous than is the worship of Christ in Christendom ; and if they worship Her through images, so do the Roman Catholics also. Of course, there are Protestants who look upon Roman Catholic Christians as idolaters, and they will, of course, pass the same un-illumined condemnation upon the Hindu Shakti-worshipper also. I have nothing to say of such criticisms. But those who really understand the inner meaning and truth of the Christian mystery of the Trinity, not as a mere dogma or creed learnt from the catechist but as a matter of personal spiritual experience, will, I think, understand the devout Shakti-worshipper much better than the deists and the rationalists, whether of India or Europe.

The cult of Radha-Krishna stands, possibly, on a yet higher ground. It is very far, indeed, from my wish to start any odious comparison between the worship of Shakti and the worship of Radha-Krishna. Such comparisons are hardly permissible in the ideal and culture of the Hindu. To the Hindu, every form of divine worship is good for those who sincerely pursue it. As all roads led to Rome in ancient Europe, so all worships in Hinduism lead to the Supreme. Shree Krishna says in the Bhagabad-Geeta :—

Ye yatha mam prapadyante tamstathaiba bhajamyaham.
Mama bartanu bartante manushyah Partha sarvashah.

"I bless each worshipper after the manner in which he worships me : mankind, O Partha, in every way pursue my own path."

And again,—

Yo yo yam yam tanum bhakta sraddhayarchitumichhati.
Tashya tashyachalam sraddham tameva bidadhamyaham.

"The different devotees who desire to worship different images with faith and devotion, I grant them firm faith in their respective images or symbols."

Sa taya sraddhaya yuktastasyaradhanamihate
Lavate cha tatah kaman maiba bihitan hitan.

"That devotee having served his own particular form with this faith, attains the fruits thereof as ordained by me."

In Hinduism, there is no particularistic emphasis such as we find in all the credal religions; there is no exclusiveness and absolutism such as characterise both Christianity and Islam. The Hindu's God is the God of all. The universe is His, and He belong to the universe. He is the Indweller in every heart, and from there directs and controls the life and evolution of all, according to their respective inner natures. To quote the Geeta once more:—

Iswara sarvabhutanam hriddeshe
Arjuna tishthati
Bhramayan sarvabhutani yantra-
rudena mayaya.

"Oh Arjuna, the Lord is seated in the heart of all creatures; and is revolving them as if upon a wheel, with His *Maya*."

This *Maya* is *Prakriti*. It is really the law of being of different objects and persons. It is the specific law of individual life and evolution. And the particularities of the religious life and ordinances of each individual are really determined by their individual law of being. This is the real *dharma* of each individual. This is his own special religion or law. This is what the Geeta calls—*swadharma*. And it is in reference to this special and specific personal law of being which constitutes the inner individuality and personality of different humans, that Shree Krishna declared in the Geeta that it is far more preferable even to die in the pursuit of this law or *dharma* than to seek the easier or even the higher law of another person. And in view of this universality of Hinduism no worship or culture can be condemned. His or her own law or *dharma*, the disciplines and worships suited to his or her inner nature, are the best for every man or woman. But yet when viewed from the stand-point of the whole or the universal, there are distinctions of superior and inferior between one form and another. This claim to superiority is not individualistic or sectarian but universal.

The Krishna-Cult

And it is from this universal stand-point that I say that the Krishna cult stands upon a much higher ground spiritually and philosophically than the other Hindu cults. In the first place, we have here a much firmer grasp of the philosophy of the Absolute than in any other Hindu system. Krishna is not the Undifferentiated Absolute, so familiar to the student of popular Monism associated with the name of Samkara. He is not the Brahman of the earlier Upanishads. He is not something like the Pure Being of your own Hegelians, which, as Hegel himself said, is equal to Pure Nothing. This is the Absolute of which our own Upanishads declared that they could posit neither being nor non-being. We cannot say that It is, we cannot say that It is not. This Brahman of the Upanishads, the worshippers of Shree Krishna say, is only an effulgence of the body of Krishna, Brahman is, in other words, only an aspect of the Reality, but not the fullness thereof. That full Reality is Shree Krishna.

Krishna is a Person. or rather, more correctly speaking, He is the one and the only Person in the universe. The human personalities are only a faint and distant shadow of His Divine Personality. And He eternally realises His Divine and Absolure Personality through an eternal process of self-differentiation. I have tried to explain briefly what this self-differentiation means in a previous letter, and will not, therefore, repeat that explanation here. This process of the eternal self-differentiation of the Absolute is called in our literature ***nitya leela*** or the eternal sport of the Lord. And in this Divine *Leela*, Radha is the eternal Partner of Shree Krishna. Radha is the Eternally Differentiated Self of Shree Krishna. Radha is, therefore, neither absolutely different from, nor absolutely identical with Krishna. Their mutual relation is one of "inconceivable difference in identity and identity in difference." It is called in Sanskrit *achintyabhedabheda*. Both this differentiation and this identification are moments in the eternnl process of Reason and Love. And it is in and through this eternal process of self-differentiation that Krishna or the Absolute – the *Parama-tattva*— the Supreme Reality as He is called in our literature, realises His personality and becomes the Person. And in this eternal process of Reason and Love, in the very Being of the Absolute, Radha as the momentarily differentiated Self of the Absolute, is also Herself a Person. And it is in and through the Personality of Radha that Krishna reaches and realises His own Personality. Apart from Radha, Krishna is only Pure Being, as the Hegelians would perhaps say. It is *Nirguna* Brahman or the Abstract Universal of our own Upanishads.

There is, as I already pointed out in a previous letter, very close affinity between the fundamental philosophy of Christianity and that of the Krishna cult of India. What Christ is in the Christian dogma, that is Radha in our Vaishnavism. There is, however, a very fundamental difference between Christianity and Vaishnavism in regard to the actual constitution of their respective Deity. Krishna does not stand for Christ, but for the Father of the Christian

Trinity. Krishna is the Absolute, but not the Absolute of metaphysical abstraction. He is the Eternally Self-Differentiated Absolute, realising His Personality through this Eternal Self-Differentiation. The Father is also the same Absolute, the same Person, realising His Personality through the same eternal method of Self-Differentiation. But notwithstanding this, the Father of the Christian Trinity is only one of the Three Persons of that Trinity, and not the whole Trinity. In Vaishnavic consciousness Krishna is not a part, not a moment, not an aspect of the Absolute, but the Absolute Itself —Eternally Self-Realised. Krishna is Bhagavan, the Absolute Person. He is, what in our modern phraseology would perhaps be called, the Concrete Universal. We seem to miss somewhat this concrete character in the Father of the Christian Trinity. The Concrete Universal in Christian consciousness is not the Father but the Son, not God but Christ. In our Vaishnavism, it is Krishna who is the Concrete Universal, and not Radha.

And it is this concrete conception of Krishna which fundamentally differentiates our Krishna cult from Christianity. There is not even the suspicion of any *form* in the Father of the Christian Trinity. The Hindu Vaishnavas openly attribute *form* to Shree Krishna, It is, of course, not a physical form. The form of Shree Krishna in Vaishnavic art is not real but only symbolic. So is also the form of Radha. Truly speaking, neither Krishna nor Radha has any material or sensuous form. Pure spiritual emotions, we are repeatedly told in Vaishnavic teachings, are the constituents of the Body of Radha. It is a spiritual body, realised in the spirit of the devotee, in his own inner and enlightened emotions, and not something carnal that can be cognised by the outer senses. So also is the Body of Shree Krishna. It is spiritual, and not material, rational and not physical.

What this spiritual *form* of Shree Krishna is. it is impossible for those who are not highly advanced in Vaishnavic culture, to think or imagine. It is revealed not to the outer eye, but in deep trance, in moments of great spiritual exaltation, when the outer senses having been absolutely quieted down, and the inner spiritual faculties having thereby been completely freed from all sensuous contacts and impulses, the soul sees with its own refined organs its own Lord and Lover. The experience is absolutely supersensuous and spiritual. But when the mind comes back to itself, at the close of the beatific vision, and is thus related once more to the outer world of sense-forms and sense-sounds, it recalls the inner spiritual experience, by associating it with outer things that represent and resemble it most closely. It is these outer remembrances that create the symbolic forms not only of Shree Krishna but also of all the numerous spiritual beings that are worshipped by the Hindus. These outer forms, visible to the natural eye, are not the real *forms* of the divine beings, but are only something purely mnemonic of their inner spiritual presence. Even so it is with the usual figures of Shree Krishna. This is purely mnemonic. You and I see in these only physical colours and contours ; but not having had any previous spiritual experience, we cannot naturally realise their real spiritual significance.

Shree Chaitanya Mahaprabhu, the *Avatara* of Nadeeya or Navadveepa (sixteenth century), in his discussion with Prakasananda, the well-known Vedantin of Benares, declared : —

Brahma shavda mukhya arthe kahe Bhagavan
Chidaisvarya paripoorna anoordha saman.
Tanhar bibhuti deha sav chidakar
Chidbibhuti acchhadiya kahe nirakar.

"The specific meaning of Brhman is Bhagavan, who is possessed of absolute spiritual powers, and has neither equal nor superior. His manifestations and His Body are all of spiritual form ; ignoring these spiritual forms and manifestations, they call Him formless."

The "Form" of Krishna

You will see from this that the forms which the Hindus attribute to the Supreme are not so gross or material as these naturally appear to the uninitiated stranger. It appears so even to many of our own people, who have not had the profound spiritual training and experiences of the saint and the devotee. There is no suspicion of any gross materialistic conception in regard to the Absolute in our Upanishads. Yet these very Upanishads speak of the Absolute as having what may be called the quintessence of the quality of the different senses, though without the sense-organs. He has no eye, but has the very quintessence of the quality of vision ; no ear but the very quintessence of the quality of audition ; no olfactory organ, but the very quintessence of the quality of smelling ; and so also in regard to all the other senses. This seems to me to be the real meaning of the text :—

Sarvendriya gunabhasam sarvendriya vivarjitam.

And the irresistible logic of thought that drove Hindu speculations to posit this sense-quality, without the sense-organs, in the Supreme, seems to have been this. When you say that God knows all, the question arises, does He or does

He not know all our sense-experiences? If He does, how is it possible, unless He has, not the outer physical senses, but something that possesses the essential quality of these organs? In other words, omniscience cannot be attributed to the Deity without positing a sensorium in His Own Being. At least it is impossible to accept His omniscience, in any system of Natural Theology, except upon the hypothesis that God has a sensorium. It is really the sensorium which is of "the quintessence of the quality of the senses." And if you grant a sensorium to the Supreme, you must also grant Him an adequate object for it. In other words, you must grant One Subject and One Object, One Enjoyer and One Object to enjoy, One Will and One Object upon which that Will eternally operates, in the very Being of the Supreme, as part of His Unity. And both these,—the Subject and the Object, the Enjoyer and the Enjoyed, the Worker and the Worked, both these terms of correlation must be co-equal and co-existent, co-infinite and co-eternal. This, at least, is how the Hindu Vaishnava must have evidently speculated, when he conceived Shree Krishna as not absolutely "formless" but possessing only "spiritual forms." In the Ultimate Reality, as seized by Vaishnavic experience,—in the *Parama-Tattva* as it is called,—Krishna is the

Subject, Radha the Object. Radha is not absolutely separated from Krishna ; nor are the two absolutely united. There is perpetual union and separation between them. As soon as the two are united they separate ; and as soon as they are separated, they unite. And out of this endless play of separation and union, flow all the various emotional moods and experiences which constitute the very soul and essence of the highest beatific enjoyments of the Vaishnava devotees. It is because of this Mystery of the Krishna-Radha relation, that the deepest Vaishnavic experience calls Krishna *Nikhhila-rasamritamoorti*, the embodiment of all the emotions and all the beatitudes. Krishna is also called *Sacchidananda-vigraha*,– which may be rendered into English as the Form of Truth, Intelligence and Bliss. And all these clearly indicate that whether we are able to understand and realise these mysteries or not, the religion of the Hindu is, after all, not at all so gross as ignorant and unimaginative strangers from Europe or America often try to make it out. There are deep mysteries here, just as you have in the dogmas and doctrines of Christianity ; and if these mysteries of Christianity do not make that religion gross and superstitious, why should the mysteries of Hinduism make it so ? The profoundest significance of Vaishnavism or the cult of Shree Krishna lies, however. in its intense and most pronounced note of humanity. In some sense, it may perhaps be said that of all the Hindu deities Shree Krishna is the least supernatural. Of course, there are numerous manifestations of Shree Krishna, called his *avataras* or incarnations ; and some of these are non-human, or a combination of the human and the non-human. But these are his descent or *avatara* in the process of either cosmic or historic evolution. The cosmic character of his incarnation, or more correctly speaking, descent—for that is the true English rendering of the Sanskrit term *avatara*—is manifest in the earlier forms of the Fish, the Tortoise, and the Boar, which Shree Krishna is said to have assumed. His manifestation as Nri-simha or the Man-Lion, has also an evident cosmic meaning. But all his later manifestations, as Rama, during the Ramayana epoch, or as Shree Krishna during the Mahabharata epoch, all these are distinct human manifestations. Indeed, the Vaishnavas believe that the real and permanent "form" of Shree Krishna is the Divine Human form. His own "form" is the very spiritual prototype of the perfected human figure. The constituent elements of it are spiritual, and not carnal, but the type is human.

In our highest emotional experiences,

especially in our experience of love, when it "passes beyond the individual and loses itself in the Infinite", do we contemplate and enjoy mere flesh ? Or, rather, on the countrary, do we not feel and realise that the form of the beloved alone is there present in our spiritual vision, but not at all his or her flesh ? In these moments of ecstatic love, the carnal melts imperceptibly into the spiritual, the mere human into the divine. Those who have these experiences, and believe that our love in its highest from is something essentially divine, will perhaps find it somewhat easy to appreciate and enter into the spirit of the high Vaishnavic conception of the real *rupa* or form of Sree Krishna. Now, this word *rupa* in Sanskrit is very significant. It is but very imperfectly rendered by the English word form. *Rupa* does not convey any idea of dimensions as the word form in English does. The spirit has no dimensions, but it has *rupa*. *Rupa* means really expression. Our emotions have no dimensions but expressions or *rupa*. When, therefore, the Vaishnava speaks of the "form" of his Lord, he does not mean by the term any material concept whatever. No Hindu, really, cherishes such gross notions about his Deity or about any Deity whatever. The soul of man is not material, but a spiritual substance. Yet whenever we individualise this soul, and speak of it as that of John or Martha, of Rama or Lachmee, we attribute some note or mark, something by which one soul may be distinguished from another. Are these marks and notes physical or non-physical? If you say they are physical, then either there is no such thing as soul at all or that after death when this physicul limitation is removed, there remains absolutely nothing by which one soul can be distinguished from another. But if you accept both the existence of what is called the soul and its immortality, then you must accept this also that this soul has a form or, more correctly speaking, a *rupa* of its own, which is not carnal or physical, but spiritual. It is this spiritual *rupa* or form which distinguishes one soul from another in the spirit-world, when at death, all their bodily characters are destroyed. And if this is admitted,—and I do not see, my child, how one can avoid this consistently with one's faith in soul and immortality,—in the sense of the continuation after death of the human individuality,—then, it will also have to be conceded as perfectly reasonable, even where one may find it hard to conceive it,—that the Supreme too may have a form or *rupa* of His own. Of course, the question does not arise with those who do not believe in a Personal Godhead. To the school of Absolute Monism, to those who accept only *Nirguna* Brahman as true, and dismiss *Saguna* Brahman as unreal and illusory,—those who worship - if worship it may at all be called — *Nirguna* Brahman or the Abstract Univeral only, to them there is no need of positing any such "form" in the Absolute. These do not believe in a real Personal God.

Personality of the Absolute

The Hindu Vaishnava believes in the Personality of the Absolute. And, consequently, he cannot help believing that the Deity has a form or *rupa* of His Own. For the very idea of personality involves distinction and differentiation. The differentiation may not be abiding and absolute. In fact, neither in our experiences of our own personality nor in our conception of the Divine Personality, is there any such abiding and absolute differentiation or duality. Every differentiation is followed immediately by integration ; every duality, immediately it is established, is subsumed in a higher and more perfected unity. So the differentiation and duality absolutely necessary for the Personality of the Godhead is not abiding and absolute but only a mere moment in the Divine Consciousness and Being. But still it is there. It is real, and not illusory. If this differentiation be not real, then the

Personality of the Godhead must also of necessity be itself unreal and illusory, mere *mayic* not *paramarthic.* The Hindu school of Absolute Monism actually hold this very view of the Personality of God. They regard it as due to *Maya.* Isvara, the Personal God of the Samkara Vedanta is, therefore, mere *mayic* as much as this phenomenal world. And in the highest state of beatitude this Isvara passes out, like all other dualities and illusions, and the consciousness of the One-without-a-Second, of the undifferentiated Unity alone remains. If you are a Monist of this class, if all your worships and prayers are mere spiritual disciplines of the same class fundamentally as your baths and ablutions, that is,—are only means to an end and not an end unto themselves,—if you believe that when the spirit is purified by these means, and the understanding is finally able to rest in the sense of the Unity, there will be no need for these lower and kindergarten cultures, then you may well and legitimately dismiss the Vaishnavic conception of the eternal and abiding *rupa* or form of the Supreme as false and fanciful. But not otherwise, my child. At the end, when you have reached the final beatitude, will your personality be merged in the Being of the Absolute? Or, will it remain differentiated from Him as now,—differentiated in being only, but united in love and will? Is love of God a privilege of the saved as it is the duty of those who are in bondage of the flesh and the world? If so, how will they love and serve the Lord from eternity to eternity, unless there are notes and marks that differentiate the Lord from His servants and devotees? These are queries that cannot be summarily set aside by those who desire to be truly rational and consistent in their faiths and practices.

The Vaishnava Hindu did not brush these aside. He boldly faced them. And realising the imperious necessity of Reason to posit a *rupa* or form in the Divine to justify His personality, he unhesitatingly declared that the Deity is not without *rupa* or form, but that He has a specific *rupa* or Form of His Own. It is not a carnal *rupa*, not a material form, not a form that has dimensions, nor a *rupa* that has physical colours and contours, but a pure, an invisible, an immaterial *rupa* or form. His *rupa* is spiritual. His form is of the elements of Pure Reason.

The Three Gunas

And we have the nearest approach to Divine *Rupa* in the *rupa* of the perfected human. But you will find it exceedingly difficult to clearly realise what the perfected human form is, without previously understanding the Hindu philosophy of what are called the three *gunas*. These three *gunas* are the very constituent elements of the universe. All that is, whether living or non-living, whether what we call material or what we call spiritual,—is really a permutation and combination of these. According to the Sankhya system of philosophy, Nature or the *Pradhana* as it is called, in its unmanifested state, prior to the beginning of creation, is only a condition of the equilibrium of these *gunas*. It is only when this equilibrium is disturbed that the process of cosmic evolution starts. Hence whatever is in the universe has these three *gunas* or properties, in certain permutations and combinations. The analysis, by means of which the Hindu mind arrived at these three *gunas* or properties as the root-elements of the universe, is not physical but psychological. The *gunas* are, therefore, not properties of matter but those of mind. They even exist in a state of perfect equilibrium in the very Being of the Supreme, according to Vaishnavic philosophy, when at dissolution or *pralaya*, creation is merged in the Creator. At the beginning of the next creative process, these once more break out into differentiation, and their equilibrium is lost.

These three qualities are,—*Sattva*, *Rajas* and *Tamas*. *Sattva* is the quality of Illumination and Godness. It is the true spiritual quality. *Rajas* is the quality of Desire and Activity. *Tamas* is the quality of Ignorance and Inertia. These are variously present in all. Even the gods are controlled by these three qualities. *Sattva*, you will see, is essentially the highest spiritual quality. *Rajas* is essentially a mental or intellectual quality. *Tamas* is a gross animal quality. An excess of *Tamas* over both *Rajas* and *Sattva*, means ignorance and inertia, mere animalism and verminonsity. An excess of *Rajas* in the composition of any person means inordinate desire for enjoyment and possession, and constant conflicts between rivals and competitors for these. An excess of *Sattva* in the composition of any one indicates his superior spirituality. Such a person is always self-illumined and self-collected, free from all the angry passions that characterise the two lower classes, lives in a perpetual consciousness of the Spiritual and the Universal. His body is perfectly attuned to the highest laws of love and bliss, and his whole being is perfectly attuned to the very Being of the Supreme. In the highest stage of the development of *Sattva* or the quality of Illumination and Godness, the man becomes absolutely possessed by his God. His body becomes, so to say, the very expression of the pure spiritual energy of the Divine.

Having been purified by the psycho-physical cultures of which I have already spoken, his body losses all its animalities, and becomes a perfect instrument for the expression of Divine Energy. His mind becomes a perfect receiver and transmitter of Divine Thought, his heart of Divine Emotions, and his will of the Will of God. Thus perfected, the human becomes divine, the individual becomes the universal. In such a man we see, even with our eyes, that which the eye cannot truly see, and realise with our intellect what transcends the intellectual. It is these men and women whose *Rajas* and *Tamas* have been absolutely overwhelmed by the excess of the quality of *Sattva*, who give us a glimpse of what we see, in moments of the most exalted beatitudes, as human perfection. It is such perfected human who slightly reveals what the Vaishnava worships as the *Rupa* or Form of his Lord.

Man Becomes Divine

We have, thus, in the higher thoughts and ideals of the Krishna cult in India, a strange apotheosis of the human, such as is not found perhaps in any other religion. Of course, I do not forget that higher Christianity has also tried to do this to some extent. But while the utmost that Christianity has done has been simply to apotheosise the spiritual in man, Vashnavism has sought to apotheosise even the physical in him. All flesh is evil, said Latin Christianity. All flesh is illusory, said Hindu Vedantism. In both Latin Christianity and Hindu Vedantism, we have, therefore, an attempt to repress the natural instincts and appetites of man in the name and interest of the higher spiritual life. But Vaishnavism has been peculiarly free from these monkish mediævalisms. In both mediæval Hinduism and mediæval Christianity, social life and relations and man's general sense-activities are only tolerated, but never whole-heartedly encouraged. Vaishnavism has been able to do this ; because of the way in which it has from of old, persistently sought to idealise and spiritualise the senses and all the human affections and relations. Vaishnavism has been able, therefore, to avoid both mediæval monasticism, and modern materialism. It condemns equally the repression of the senses and the affections of man, as well as their Godless and lustful service. Its aim is not mere regulation of the senses, but their idealisation and spiritualisation. To the truly pious Vaishnava his body is not his own, but that of his Lord Shree Krishna. The service of his body, therefore, is really service of Krishna himself. His care and regard for his own flesh is of the same character as his care for the image of his Krishna, and he seeks to cultivate the same sacred sentiments in relation to the daily service of his own physical body, as those with which he worships his Deity through his special symbol. I know of Vaishnavas who are literally lost in beatific exaltation when dressing after their daily ablutions, at the thought that the image of their own body upon the mirror before them, is really the very instrument of *leela* or sport of their Lord.

Two Aspects of Leela

This *leela* or sport of Shree Krishna has two aspects : one inner and the other outer. The inner *leela*, called in Sanskrit, *antaranga leela*, is the eternal sport of the Lord within his own being. Radha, His own self-differentiated *Prakriti*, is Krishna's partner in this inner or *antaranga leela*. This inner or *antaranga leela* stands outside the time series. It is eternal. It is also called in our literature, *aprakrita leela* or supranatural sport. There is, however, another aspect of the *leela* of the Lord. It is his outer *leela*, called also His *prakrita* or natural *leela*. In Sanskrit it is also called His *bahiranga leela*. *Bahiranga* means the outer body. This universe is the outer body of Shree Krishna. This is what is called his *Visvarupa* or Universe-Form. It was this Universe-Form of the Lord which was revealed to Arjuna at the field of Kurukshetra, of which we read in the Geeta. The *bahiranga leela* of the Lord means, therefore, His *leela* or sportive manifestation in the outer cosmic life and activities, and especially in the human kingdom. This outer or *bahiranga leela* is not an absolute necessity of His being. That inner necessity is fully met by His inner *leela* of which Shree Radha is his co-partner. As the co-partner of the Lord in His inner or *antaranga leela*, Shree Radha is a necessity of the very Being of the Absolute. Shree Krishna cannot exist without Shree Radha, just as in Christian consciousness the Father cannot exist without the Son, God without Christ. *Purusha* and *Prakriti*, Krishna and Radha, Father and Son, God and Christ, – cannot exist without one another. The one without the other is unreal, a mere abstraction. But the same necessity does not exist in regard to the *bahiranga* or the outer cosmic *leela* or sport. The Absolute is full and complete in His own being. The outer phenomenal world is not at all a necessity of His Being. This is the common Vaishnavic and Christian view. The world is not necessary for God. But He is necessary for the world. He has no need, really, of us : we alone have need of Him. Our relations with Him are not necessary like those of Radha in Vaishnavic consciousness, or of Christ in Christian consciousness. In Christianity Humanity is God's, not upon its own right, but through Christ. Mankind are sons of God, not on their own right but, through adoption, in Christ. Similarly in Vashnavic consciousness, the *jeeva*—the common name for all intelligent creation, including both human and non-human, —is Krishna's, not upon the *jeeva's* own right, but through His *Prakriti*, by adoption. We are not, according to real Hindu Theism, as distinguished from the Monism of the Samkara-Vedanta School,—the image of God, but that of His *Prakriti*. Not Krishna but Radha is our prototype. We are not *Purushas* but *Prakritis*. *Purusha* is one: and though His specific *Prakriti* also is One, yet there are an infinity of inferior *Prakritis*. Radha is Krishna's own real superior *Prakriti* : we humans are also His superior or *Para-prakritis*, but only by adoption, so to say, through Radha. As in His own inner being, Krishna is eternally engaged in His inner *leela* with Radha as his co-partner, so in this outer cosmic *leela*, we humans are the co-partners of the *leela* of the Lord. Our bodies and our senses are the instruments and vehicles of His sport. The purification of the body means, thus, the brightening of the instruments of the sport of Krishna. Krishna enjoys this world of senses in and through our senses. The due cultivation of the sense-life is, therefore, the service not of the senses, but of Krishna himself. One of the definitions of *Bhakti* or love of the Lord in Vaishnavism is, therefore, this, namely, that it is the service of the Director of the senses with the senses themselves. Krishna as the Indweller, is the Direetor of all our sense-activities. His service, through the sense-activities is, therefore, a service of love.

But as long as we have a sense of ownership over our own body and our senses so long Shree Krishna cannot use and enjoy these as the instruments and vehicles of His own *leela* or sport. His *leela* or sport, whether in His own inner being or in this outer creation, whether it be *antaranga* or *bahiranga*, is always with Shree Radha, and not with any other being. Before our bodies and our senses can be used by Shree Krishna as instruments and vehicles of His *leela*, they must cease to be ours, and become completely Radha's. We must cherish absolutely no sense of proprietorship over these. This sense of ownness over one's body and the senses is, according to Vaishnavic ideals, the greatest of all sins. To deny them their legitimate play and fulfilment, to seek to repress their natural activities by cruel penance and monkish renunciation, is also equally sinful. To torture the body under a mistaken ideal of religion and piety is to torture Krishna himself. To use it for gross and selfish enjoyments is to usurp the very rights and liberties of Shree Krishna himself. The Vaishnava desirous of cultivating the love of the Lord must carefully avoid both these extremes. This is the negative side of the higher Vaishnavic culture. The positive side consists in the absolute dedication of the body and the senses to the service of Krishna. The senses are not ours but Krishna's. It is He alone who has a right to their use and enjoyment. But He uses them and enjoys them not as our own, but as Shree Radha's. The devotee, in what people call his own sense-life and sense-activities, is merely a blessed witness of the *leela* or sport of the Lord. It is not the *leela* between Shree Krishna and himself, but between Shree Krishna and Shree Radha. He sees and enjoys in his own body this Radha-Krishna *leela*. This is the highest Vaishnava ideal. Our self is not directly the partner of this supreme *leela*, but simply a witness of it. As in the deepest Christian experience, the Christian devotee is not the direct participant in the transcendental colloquy between the Father and the Son, but is only a witness of it ; as the loftiest aspiration of the Christian saint is not to join that eternal colloquy between the Father and the Son, but simply to stand from eternity to eternity by the Throne of Glory and there see the Father in the Son and the Son in the Father, and rapturously listen to their blessed colloquy : even so the highest Vaishnavic ideal is to simply witness this Radha-Krishna *leela* within and without. In his sense-life he seeks to realise this Radha-Krishna *leela*. It is thus that he loses the conceit of ownership over these. It is by this means that in higher Vaishnavic culture even the very flesh is purified, spiritualised, idealised and universalised. It is here that we must seek for the secret of that supreme vicariousness of even the sense-life of our highest Vaishnavic devotees. But in this higher Vaishnavic culture, not only are the body and the senses spiritualised and universalised, but all the social relations are also equally idealised and universalised.

The Nine Rasas

The Vishnavas seek to realise and enjoy the Supreme as what they call *Nikhilarasamrita-moorti* or the "form" of all the *rasas* and all *amrita*. These ***rasas*** are the emotions. They are the objects of what is called the æsthetic faculty in European literature and philosophy. The analysis of this faculty in Hindu thought is more thorough than in European thought.

This æsthetic faculty is called in our literature the *ranjinee vritti*. It is what may be called the faculty of enjoyment as well as the colouring faculty. *Ranjan* in Sanskrit means both to enjoy and to colour. And the so-called æsthetic faculty does both in regard to our intellectual life. It gives enjoyments to us, as well as lends colour to all our objects of knowledge. The *rasas* are the objects of this faculty. These *rasas* are really the emotions. These according to our literature and philosophy are nine in number. They are :—(i) *Sringara* : also called *adi* or the original *rasa*. It may be rendered into English by love, but love with a clear sex-reference. It is called *adi* or the original *rasa* because it lies at the very root of creation. (ii) *Veera* : the word is radically the same as the Latin *vir*, and means the emotion of courage and valour, that which we feel at the sight of acts of physical bravery. (iii) *Karuna* : pity and compassion. (iv) *Advuta* : the sense of wonder. Literally, it means the emotion that is quickened in the presence of something that had never happened before. (v) *Hasya* : laughter. (vi) *Bhayanaka* : fear. (vii) *Bibhatsa* : or the sense of the terrible. (viii) *Raudra* : or anger. (ix) *Shanta* : or absolute quietude. These are the nine *rasas*. And the Universal as the Source and Substance of these various emotions, is what the Vaishnavas seek to realise and enjoy as *Nikhilarasamritamoorti*. It is as the Universal Source and Substance of all our various emotions that the Vaishnava realises Shree Krishna in the moods and expressions of his own physical and sense life.

Vaishnavic Contribution to Hindu Aesthetics

But to these nine *rasas* of Hindu æsthetics, the Vaishnavas add four more that are distinctly human and social emotions. The nine *rasas* enumerated above are the common experience of all *jeeva*. We have them in common with our brother animals in what is called the lower animal kingdom. But these four specific Vaishnavic *rasas* are confined absolutely to the human kingdom, and are the result of our social relations. These are :—(i) *Dasya*, or the emotion of the devoted servant or valet towards his lord and master ; (ii) *Sakhya*, or the complex emotions that find play in our deepest friendships ; (iii) *Vatsalya*, or the parental feeling ; and (iv) *Madhur*, or the deep emotions that find play in our congugal life and the true romance of the man-and-wife relation. Shree Krishna is not only the source and substance of the lower *rasas* that rise through our contact and relations with Nature and the lower animal kingdom but also of all the emotions that find play in our specific human relations. Krishna, to the Vaishnava, is thus Lord, Friend, Father and Son, and Lover and Love. All our human relations are mere reflex of these relations that exist in Shree Krishna Himself as part of His Own-Being. Shree Krishna, thus, spiritualises all these social relations even as He spiritualises our physical activities and enjoyments. In his master the devout Vaishnava, thus, sees his Krishna. In his personal friend he realises and relishes Krishna as Friend. In his son and father, in his daughter and mother, he realises and serves his Krishna. In his conjugal life and relation he realises and enjoys the highest, the depest love of Krishna.

It is thus that in Hindu Vaishnavism, we have a more thorough, more concrete, at once a more real and a more ideal presentation of the Universal than perhaps we have in any other culture. In Vaishnavism the innate sense of the Spiritual and the Universal of the Indo-Aryan Race-Consciousness seems to have found its loftiest and deepest expression.

If, my child. you want to visualise the Soul of India, you must seek and find it in Shree Krishna.